Layers of Learning

Year Two • Unit Fifteen

Mongols
Caucasus
Gases & Kinetic Theory
Fun With Poetry

Published by HooDoo Publishing
United States of America
© 2014 Layers of Learning
Copies of maps or activities may be made for a particular family or classroom.
ISBN 978-1495315695

If you wish to reproduce or print excerpts of this publication, please contact us at contact@layers-of-learning.com for permission. Thank you for respecting copyright laws.

Units At A Glance: Topics For All Four Years of the Layers of Learning Program

1	History	Geography	Science	The Arts
1	Mesopotamia	Maps & Globes	Planets	Cave Paintings
2	Egypt	Map Keys	Stars	Egyptian Art
3	Europe	Global Grids	Earth & Moon	Crafts
4	Ancient Greece	Wonders	Satellites	Greek Art
5	Babylon	Mapping People	Humans in Space	Poetry
6	The Levant	Physical Earth	Laws of Motion	List Poems
7	Phoenicians	Oceans	Motion	Moral Stories
8	Assyrians	Deserts	Fluids	Rhythm
9	Persians	Arctic	Waves	Melody
10	Ancient China	Forests	Machines	Chinese Art
11	Early Japan	Mountains	States of Matter	Line & Shape
12	Arabia	Rivers & Lakes	Atoms	Color & Value
13	Ancient India	Grasslands	Elements	Texture & Form
14	Ancient Africa	Africa	Bonding	African Tales
15	First North Americans	North America	Salts	Creative Kids
16	Ancient South America	South America	Plants	South American Art
17	Celts	Europe	Flowering Plants	Jewelry
18	Roman Republic	Asia	Trees	Roman Art
19	Christianity	Australia & Oceania	Simple Plants	Instruments
20	Roman Empire	You Explore	Fungi	Composing Music

2	History	Geography	Science	The Arts
1	Byzantines	Turkey	Climate & Seasons	Byzantine Art
2	Barbarians	Ireland	Forecasting	Illumination
3	Islam	Arabian Peninsula	Clouds & Precipitation	Creative Kids
4	Vikings	Norway	Special Effects	Viking Art
5	Anglo Saxons	Britain	Wild Weather	King Arthur Tales
6	Charlemagne	France	Cells and DNA	Carolingian Art
7	Normans	Nigeria	Skeletons	Canterbury Tales
8	Feudal System	Germany	Muscles, Skin, & Cardiopulmonary	Gothic Art
9	Crusades	Balkans	Digestive & Senses	Religious Art
10	Burgundy, Venice, Spain	Switzerland	Nerves	Oil Paints
11	Wars of the Roses	Russia	Health	Minstrels & Plays
12	Eastern Europe	Hungary	Metals	Printmaking
13	African Kingdoms	Mali	Carbon Chem	Textiles
14	Asian Kingdoms	Southeast Asia	Non-metals	Vivid Language
15	Mongols	Caucasus	Gases	Fun With Poetry
16	Medieval China & Japan	China	Electricity	Asian Arts
17	Pacific Peoples	Micronesia	Circuits	Arts of the Islands
18	American Peoples	Canada	Technology	Indian Legends
19	The Renaissance	Italy	Magnetism	Renaissance Art I
20	Explorers	Caribbean Sea	Motors	Renaissance Art II

3	History	Geography	Science	The Arts
1	Age of Exploration	Argentina and Chile	Classification & Insects	Fairy Tales
2	The Ottoman Empire	Egypt and Libya	Reptiles & Amphibians	Poetry
3	Mogul Empire	Pakistan & Afghanistan	Fish	Mogul Arts
4	Reformation	Angola & Zambia	Birds	Reformation Art
5	Renaissance England	Tanzania & Kenya	Mammals & Primates	Shakespeare
6	Thirty Years' War	Spain	Sound	Baroque Music
7	The Dutch	Netherlands	Light & Optics	Baroque Art I
8	France	Indonesia	Bending Light	Baroque Art II
9	The Enlightenment	Korean Pen.	Color	Art Journaling
10	Russia & Prussia	Central Asia	History of Science	Watercolors
11	Conquistadors	Baltic States	Igneous Rocks	Creative Kids
12	Settlers	Peru & Bolivia	Sedimentary Rocks	Native American Art
13	13 Colonies	Central America	Metamorphic Rocks	Settler Sayings
14	Slave Trade	Brazil	Gems & Minerals	Colonial Art
15	The South Pacific	Australasia	Fossils	Principles of Art
16	The British in India	India	Chemical Reactions	Classical Music
17	Boston Tea Party	Japan	Reversible Reactions	Folk Music
18	Founding Fathers	Iran	Compounds & Solutions	Rococo
19	Declaring Independence	Samoa and Tonga	Oxidation & Reduction	Creative Crafts I
20	The American Revolution	South Africa	Acids & Bases	Creative Crafts II

4	History	Geography	Science	The Arts
1	American Government	USA	Heat & Temperature	Patriotic Music
2	Expanding Nation	Pacific States	Motors & Engines	Tall Tales
3	Industrial Revolution	U.S. Landscapes	Energy	Romantic Art I
4	Revolutions	Mountain West States	Energy Sources	Romantic Art II
5	Africa	U.S. Political Maps	Energy Conversion	Impressionism I
6	The West	Southwest States	Earth Structure	Impressionism II
7	Civil War	National Parks	Plate Tectonics	Post-Impressionism
8	World War I	Plains States	Earthquakes	Expressionism
9	Totalitarianism	U.S. Economics	Volcanoes	Abstract Art
10	Great Depression	Heartland States	Mountain Building	Kinds of Art
11	World War II	Symbols and Landmarks	Chemistry of Air & Water	War Art
12	Modern East Asia	The South States	Food Chemistry	Modern Art
13	India's Independence	People of America	Industry	Pop Art
14	Israel	Appalachian States	Chemistry of Farming	Modern Music
15	Cold War	U.S. Territories	Chemistry of Medicine	Free Verse
16	Vietnam War	Atlantic States	Food Chains	Photography
17	Latin America	New England States	Animal Groups	Latin American Art
18	Civil Rights	Home State Study	Instincts	Theater & Film
19	Technology	Home State Study II	Habitats	Architecture
20	Terrorism	America in Review	Conservation	Creative Kids

Unit 2-15 Printable Pack

This unit includes printables at the end. To make life easier for you we also created digital printable packs for each unit. To retrieve your printable pack for Unit 2-15, please visit

www.layers-of-learning.com/digital-printable-packs/

Put the printable pack in your shopping cart and use this coupon code:

8602UNIT2-15

Your printable pack will be free.

Layers of Learning Introduction

This is part of a series of units in the Layers of Learning homeschool curriculum, including the subjects of history, geography, science, and the arts. Children from 1st through 12th can participate in the same curriculum at the same time – family school style.

The units are intended to be used in order as the basis of a complete curriculum (once you add in a systematic math, reading, and writing program). You begin with Year 1 Unit 1 no matter what ages your children are. Spend about 2 weeks on each unit. You pick and choose the activities within the unit that appeal to you and read the books from the book list that are available to you or find others on the same topic from your library. We highly recommend that you use the timeline in every history section as the backbone. Then flesh out your learning with reading and activities that highlight the topics you think are the most important.

Alternatively, you can use the units as activity ideas to supplement another curriculum in any order you wish. You can still use them with all ages of children at the same time.

When you've finished with Year One, move on to Year Two, Year Three, and Year Four. Then begin again with Year One and work your way through the years again. Now your children will be older, reading more involved books, and writing more in depth. When you have completed the sequence for the second time, you start again on it for the third and final time. If your student began with Layers of Learning in 1st grade and stayed with it all the way through she would go through the four year rotation three times, firmly cementing the information in her mind in ever increasing depth. At each level you should expect increasing amounts of outside reading and writing. High schoolers in particular should be reading extensively, and if possible, participating in discussion groups.

☺ ☺ ☺ These icons will guide you in spotting activities and books that are appropriate for the age of child you are working with. But if you think an activity is too juvenile or too difficult for your kids, adjust accordingly. The icons are not there as rules, just guides.

☺ Grades 1-4
☺ Grades 5-8
☺ Grades 9-12

Within each unit we share:
- EXPLORATIONS, activities relating to the topic;
- EXPERIMENTS, usually associated with science topics;
- EXPEDITIONS, field trips;
- EXPLANATIONS, teacher helps or educational philosophies.

In the sidebars we also include Additional Layers, Famous Folks, Fabulous Facts, On the Web, and other extra related topics that can take you off on tangents, exploring the world and your interests with a bit more freedom. The curriculum will always be there to pull you back on track when you're ready.

You can learn more about how to use this curriculum at www.layers-of-learning.com/layers-of-learning-program/

MONGOLS – CAUCASUS – GASES & KINETIC THEORY- FUN WITH POETRY

UNIT FIFTEEN

MONGOLS – CAUCASUS – GASES & KINETIC THEORY – FUN WITH POETRY

The name of peace is sweet, and the thing itself is beneficial, but there is a great difference between peace and servitude. Peace is freedom in tranquility, servitude is the worst of all evils, to be resisted not only by war, but even by death.
-Cicero, Roman Statesman

	LIBRARY LIST:
HISTORY	Search for: Mongols, Genghis Khan, Kublai Khan, Tamerlane, Golden Horde 🙂 🙂 Kublai Khan: The Emperor of Everything by Kathleen Krull. Presents the emperor in a mostly positive light. Fairly lengthy text. 🙂 Life in Genghis Khan's Mongolia by Robert Taylor. 🙂 Genghis Khan: 13th Century Mongolian Tyrant by Enid A. Goldberg and Norman Itzkowitz. From the most excellent *Horrible Histories* series. 🙂 🙂 Genghis Khan by Jacob Abbott. 🙂 🙂 The Age of Tamerlane by David Nicolle. 🙂 🙂 The Mongols by David Morgan. 🙂 The History of the Mongol Conquests by J.J. Saunders. 🙂 The Rise and Fall of the Second Largest Empire in History: How Genghis Khan's Mongols Almost Conquered the World by Thomas J. Craughwell. Short, entertaining read. 🙂 Genghis Khan's Greatest General: Subotai the Valiant by Richard A. Gabriel. About the great general who was the driving force behind most of the expansions of the Mongols during Genghis' lifetime. A military history of battles. 🙂 Genghis: Birth of an Empire by Conn Iggulden. Historical fiction, takes some liberties with the story line, but gives a good taste of what Mongol life was really like and why Genghis turned out so hard and cruel. Pre-read before you give it to your child.
GEOGRAPHY	Search for: Georgia (the country, not the U.S. state), Armenia, Azerbaijan, Caucasus 🙂 The Greedy Sparrow: An Armenian Tale by Lucine Kasbarian. 🙂 Armenia in Pictures by Bella Waters. 🙂 Legends of the Caucasus by David Hunt. 🙂 Lonely Planet: Georgia, Armenia, & Azerbaijan by John Noble, Danielle Systermans, and Michael Kohn. A guidebook about the countries.

Mongols – Caucasus – Gases & Kinetic Theory - Fun With Poetry

SCIENCE	Search for: gases, kinetic theory ☻ <u>Gases</u> by Ben Morgan. ☻ <u>The Properties of Gases</u> by Marylou Morano Kjelle. ☻ ☻ <u>Hydrogen and the Noble Gases</u> by Salvatore Tocci. ☻ <u>Gases and Their Properties</u> by Susan Meyer. ☻ <u>Gases and Their Properties</u> by Tom Jackson. ☻ <u>The Laws of Gases: Memoirs</u> by Robert Boyle and E.H. Amagat by Carl Barus, trans. The paper Boyle wrote on the laws of gases (PV=k) is only ten pages long and can be found in this volume.
THE ARTS	Search for: Any children's poetry books at your library, there should be an entire section of them. ☻ ☻ <u>The Random House Book of Poetry for Children</u> by Jack Prelutsky and Arnold Lobel. ☻ ☻ <u>A Child's Book of Poems</u> by Gyo Fujikawa. ☻ ☻ <u>The Oxford Illustrated Book of American Children's Poems</u> by Donald Hall. ☻ ☻ <u>A Child's Garden of Verses</u> by Robert Louis Stevenseon and Brian Wildsmith. ☻ ☻ ☻ <u>Poems to Learn by Heart</u> by Caroline Kennedy and Jon J. Muth. ☻ ☻ ☻ <u>Poetry for Young People: Robert Frost</u> by Gary D. Schmidt and Henri Sorensen. ☻ ☻ ☻ <u>Poetry for Young People: Maya Angelou</u> by Dr. Edwin Graves Wilson Ph.D. And Jerome Lagarrigue. ☻ ☻ ☻ <u>Poetry for Young People: Langston Hughes</u> by David Roessel, Arnold, Rampersad, and Benny Andrews. ☻ ☻ ☻ <u>A Child's Introduction to Poetry: Listen While You Learn About the Magic Words That Have Moved Mountains, Won Battles, and Made Us Laugh and Cry</u> by Michael Driscoll.

MONGOLS – CAUCASUS – GASES & KINETIC THEORY- FUN WITH POETRY

HISTORY: MONGOLS

Fabulous Fact

The Mongols were probably the most brutal people to ever live. Hitler's brutality is nothing to the treatment the Mongols dished out to their enemies. Many books soften this reality and present the Mongols as the bringers of stability and prosperity, of culture and art. They were not. In a few places they conquered they settled down and adopted the culture of the conquered and then became civilized, but their own culture was decidedly brutal, uncivilized, and backward. They destroyed prosperity, culture, and entire civilizations wherever they went. They had no regard for life at all, not even the lives of their own people.

Yet there were positive aspects of the Mongol rule as well. We'll explore some of them as well.

Fabulous Fact

Most of the information we have about Genghis Khan comes from *The Secret History of the Mongols* written for the Mongol court.

In the Middle Ages the Mongols became so powerful that they affected nearly every people and every kingdom and empire from Spain to Japan and from India to Russia. They began as separate nomadic tribes linked by ancestry, intermarriage, language, and culture. They were either Shamanistic or Buddhist. Over time they became simultaneously Shahs of Persia, Emperors of China, Tsars of Russia, Shahs of India, and Khans of Mongolia. The Mongol Empire was the largest ever in the history of the world, until the British built their empire in the 19th century.

Genghis Khan and three of his sons preparing to lay siege to a city.

Their power emerged when the disparate tribes were united under one leader, Genghis Khan, and instead of fighting with one another, they began to make war on their neighbors. Eventually as their power waned they were assimilated into the people they had conquered, except for the peoples who had remained in their Mongolian homeland.

☺ ☺ ☺ **EXPLORATION: Timeline**

All dates are AD. You will find a set of printable timeline squares at the end of this unit.

- 1125 Jin Dynasty attempts to control Mongol territory
- 1143 Mongols defeat Jin
- 1147 Jin sign peace treaty, but encourage enemy tribes to harass the Mongols
- 1161 Jin and Tatar combined defeat Mongols
- 1206 Genghis Khan is declared Great Khan, uniting all the tribes
- 1227 Genghis Khan dies, chaos ensues, then in 1229 Ogedei takes power
- 1234 Mongols defeat the Jin for the last time

MONGOLS – CAUCASUS – GASES & KINETIC THEORY - FUN WITH POETRY

- 1235-1238 Karakorum is built
- 1240 Lands of the Rus fall to the Mongols
- 1241 Combined army of Teutonic Knights, Hospitallers, Poles, Moravians, and Templars defeated at the Sajo River. Mongols then marched on to Vienna.
- Dec 1241 Khan dies and all captains and leaders are recalled to the capital, halting the invasion of Europe
- 1260-1264 War of succession splits the empire
- 1264 Kublai Khan rules from China
- 1295 Western Mongols begin to accept Islam, giving up their traditional beliefs and way of life.
- 1304 Empire is briefly reunited
- 1368 Chinese overthrow Yuan Dynasty (Mongol rulers of China)

🙂 🙂 🙂 **EXPLORATION: On the Eve of the Mongol Destruction**

At the end of this unit you will find a blank map "On the Eve of the Mongol Destruction" to color.

The colored map below shows all the empires and kingdoms and some of the tribal groups of the area affected most by the Mongols. This is the year 1200 AD and the Mongols have not yet consolidated their rule over their own tribes. But in less than 30 years they will rule over vast areas of Asia. In about sixty years they will rule from Vienna to the China Sea, most of India, all of China, and most of the Middle East.

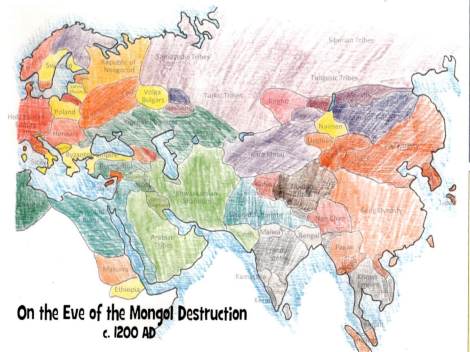

On the Eve of the Mongol Destruction
c. 1200 AD

Additional Layer
The Mongols never attacked a city, an army, or a people without first doing extensive spy work. Their prowess in battle was formidable, but would not have been nearly enough if they didn't already know the strengths and weaknesses of their enemies, including who might be bribed or where the walls were weakest.

What role do spy agencies have in today's world?

Additional Layer
Many of the kingdoms shown on the map are never mentioned anywhere else in this curriculum. They're not unimportant peoples, but we don't have time or space to study them as they have no lasting direct impact on the West or on world history in general. Some of them have fascinating histories. Look them up and read an article or two.

Teaching Tip
As you look up the various tribes on this map, write an index card about each one. Mount the map and the cards on a poster and include a line linking each card to its spot on the map.

Mongols – Caucasus – Gases & Kinetic Theory - Fun With Poetry

Fabulous Fact
The Naiman people have a very old tradition that their ancestors were the magi who visited the Christ child in Bethlehem. Their descendants stayed faithful to the Christian faith for centuries afterward. When Christian Naiman commanders were put in charge of Mongol armies they treated the Christians in the conquered lands with respect and reverence.

Fabulous Fact
Genghis Khan is a title. He was named Temujin at his birth.

Fabulous Fact
Noble women of the Mongols, including Borte, functioned as local rulers, and had their own land. In Mongols' minds, men went to war, women took care of things at home – everything from raising the children to running the country. Women in the Mongol world often ruled as regents or behind the scenes while their men were busy with war. This explains the condition of the Mughal Empire in India, where the only woman ever to rule in an Islamic state reigned. She was a Mongol, not an Arab.

We colored the various nations according to their religions. Shades of green depict Muslim states; shades of yellow, orange and red show Christians; browns show Buddhism; pagan or shamanistic peoples are shown in purples; and Hindu states are in gray. There is some overlap however. For example, the Buddhist state of Pagan also contained a large proportion of Hindus and a large proportion of Christians. The Ghunid Sultanate of northern India had Muslim rulers, but the people were mostly Hindu. In Japan the shoguns are Buddhists, but people are still practicing their native religion of shintoism. And the region of Kashmir was almost equally Hindu and Muslim. We colored the states according to the religion of the ruling class. Notice also that Europe is not the only Christian place in the world. Makurra and Ethiopia in Africa are Christian to this day. Surprisingly Naiman and Uyghurs were Christian, far isolated from other Christians in central Asia. Before the advent of Islam, Christianity had spread clear to China and was the dominant religion of the Middle East and North Africa. By 1200 there are still a few pockets of Christianity remaining in far flung places of the world.

☺ ☻ EXPLORATION: A Rescue

Genghis' road to greatness began with tragedy. His young bride, Borte, was kidnapped by a rival tribe, the Merkats. In order to get her back Temujin united the tribes with manipulation and intimidation into one people and went after the Merkats. He defeated them, rescued Borte, and then went on to defeat other tribes, until the Mongols were a nation and not just a bunch of warring tribes. What would you do to rescue a loved one? Write an adventure play of Genghis's rescue. Put it on with acting or puppets.

☺ ☻ EXPLORATION: Popular Support

Often nobles and aristocrats think they are the ones with all the power, but it is not always so. Temujin gained the role of Khan in spite of opposition from the nobles because he divided the spoils

Mongols – Caucasus – Gases & Kinetic Theory - Fun With Poetry

of war with his soldiers, rather than only sharing with the people in power. Also, he did not allow pillaging or raping after a battle unless it suited him and this gained the loyalty of many of the people he conquered as well, since in most cases their own rulers were nothing to be proud of. Also, there were none left alive that resisted the Khan. If a tribe surrendered peacefully they might expect to live, but if they resisted, then everyone was put to the sword, save a few slaves. Very few ever beat Genghis.

What would you do to gain the support of the people over the ruling class? Imagine you are Genghis Khan trying to gain the support of the people and solidify your power. Write a proclamation telling the people why they should support you.

☺ ☺ ☺ **EXPLORATION: Mongol Expansion**
Color a map showing the empire growing.

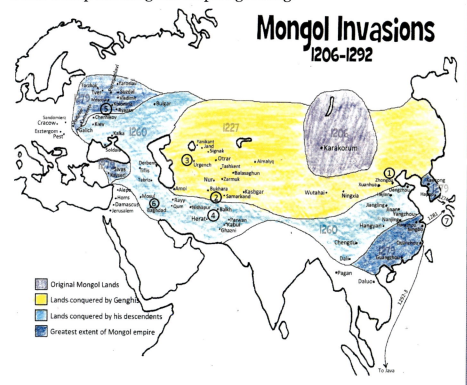

You'll find a "Mongol Invasions" map to color at the end of this unit. On the map there are numbers. Also at the end of this unit there is a numbered description "Stories of the Mongol Invasions." The numbers on the description page correspond to the numbers on the map so your kids can find the cities on the map as you describe the way the Mongols conducted their warfare. It is brutal and shocking. You can leave the descriptions out for younger kids if you wish. Every city on the map, except Karakorum, is one the Mongols took in battle, many of them brutally.

Additional Layer

Marco Polo, his uncles, and father visited Kublai Khan in his Chinese court. Learn more about Marco Polo's travels.

Additional Layer

Besides Marco Polo and family, thousands of other Europeans, most of them Italians, visited the east as traders. They used roads built and maintained and policed by the Mongols. Learn more about the Silk Road.

Additional Layer

The law was extremely harsh in the Mongol Empire, including the death penalty for many seemingly minor offenses. But the harsh measures made the land very safe. Women did not fear rape. Merchants did not fear brigands. Children did not fear kidnappers. One might walk freely anywhere in the Empire.

How are the laws of a land related to safety? How do the laws and their execution in your own land affect the safety of your family?

Mongols – Caucasus – Gases & Kinetic Theory – Fun With Poetry

Additional Layer

The Chinese invented paper money, but the Mongols perfected it, eventually leading to hyperinflation . . . how nice. Learn more about paper money, why it has value and what the dangers are in using it.

Fabulous Fact

The Mongols usually saved the skilled artisans such as architects, stone carvers, metal workers, road builders, wood carvers, potters and others to go live in Karakorum. These were not the lucky ones. They first watched their families killed, their wives and daughters raped, their sons tortured, and then were sent into a harsh brutal land far, far from their homes, their people, their cultures, and their language. They became slaves to the Khan in building his cities. The Mongols had no artisans of their own. They barely had a culture at all. They were illiterate herdsmen who lived off of yaks and goats and in tents. If they wanted cities and an empire they would have to enslave the intellects and skills of others.

☺ ☻ EXPLORATION: To Rule an Empire

To rule the new empire, Genghis had to organize his people. He divided the army into arbans (ten soldiers) within zuuns (100 soldiers) within myangans (1000 soldiers) within turmens (10,000 soldiers). He appointed capable people who had served him well to important positions, even if they had been of low class previously, and very few of his family members made the cut. Of course, most of them had united against him to depose him in the early days. And finally, he wrote a law code for his people called the Yassa. That way everyone lives by the same laws and keeps the same traditions and knows what is expected of them.

Some of Genghis' laws:

1. It is illegal to sell women.
2. No hunting during the breeding season (spring – fall).
3. Everyone may worship as they choose.
4. No stealing.
5. The poor and the churches do not pay taxes.
6. No fighting between tribes.
7. Records of the empire will be kept.
8. A supreme judge will be appointed over other judges.
9. Trade with other nations will be encouraged.
10. Every man must serve in the army.
11. No Mongols may be made slaves.
12. No one may assist a runaway slave.
13. Women own and administer all property, leaving the men free for hunting and war.
14. Most offenses are punishable by death.

Use beans or another small object to show the divisions of the army, grouped by tens and multiples of ten.

Great powerful kings often write law codes. Write your own law code, to keep handy for when you become a great ruler. It's always good to be prepared. Would you be very strict or more lenient? What would be illegal and what freedoms would you guarantee? How would you ensure a peaceful succession (something the Mongols never managed)?

☺ ☻ EXPLORATION: Yurts

Yurts (also called ger) are the round tents that Mongol nomads lived in and still live in today. You can make a model yurt from straws, metal brads, and poster board.

Mongols – Caucasus – Gases & Kinetic Theory – Fun With Poetry

1. Punch holes in the ends of 12 straws. Attach the straws together with a brad. This forms the structure of the roof.
2. Cut a piece of poster board so it is a strip about 7" wide. We used a half size sheet of poster board cut in half the long way and then attached the two strips end to end with tape to make the walls of our yurt. The whole strip needs to be about 43" long.
3. Decorate a door. Yurts are usually plain white except for the door which is made of wood and brightly painted and decorated.
4. Tape the poster board strip into a circle to make the walls.
5. Now punch 12 holes around the upper edge of your poster board circle, as evenly spaced as you can get them.
6. Insert the ends of the straws into the holes. You'll need to secure at least some of the ribs with tape to keep them in place.
7. Make a roof from triangular shaped pieces of white paper, attached in the center with another brad and taped together.
8. We just laid the paper over the roof so the kids could take it off and play with their action figures inside the yurt.

On The Web

This BBC special on the Mongols is a full length 50 minute episode.

Here is the first part:

http://youtu.be/QgYYUZGNS08

Fabulous Fact

The 1348-50 outbreak of the plague in Europe, which destroyed 1/3 of the population, was brought west from China by the Mongols. In an early form of biological warfare, the Mongols flung infected bodies over city walls under siege. Their ploy worked. Learn more about the Black Death.

Additional Layer

All males in conquered lands were liable to be drafted into the Mongol army. The Mongol tribes themselves were small and completely unable to carry on such far flung and massive war efforts on their own, let alone rule over such a vast empire. They relied on conquered men as soldiers.

Mongols – Caucasus – Gases & Kinetic Theory – Fun With Poetry

Fabulous Fact

Genghis made a lot of rules that helped his empire be a functional government, but he never did settle the question of succession, or who would rule next. He decided that upon his death, his third son, Ogedei would rule. Genghis commanded such respect that this transfer of power went peacefully. But among Ghengis' many grandsons there was already competition and positioning for power.

Ogedei died in December of 1241. The Mongol forces that had been marching through Europe, that had just soundly beaten the best knights in Christendom, suddenly halted just outside the gates of Vienna and rushed as quickly as they could back to Karakorum to attend the kurultai, elections for the next ruler. The power struggle lasted for four years of uncertainty and posturing, during which Ogedai's widow, Toregene, ruled as a regent for whoever would come next. She did her own scheming as well, favoring her son, Guruk, who was elected in time.

Guruk died in 1248, the same year he was elected. So the struggle went on.

☺ ☺ ☻ **EXPLORATIONS: Interruptions of the Political Game**

Whenever a khan died, everyone of any political importance rushed back to the capital with their soldiers. This was the law, but also they all hurried to get their guy on the throne. Successful invasions were often called off at a moments notice. Europe was saved by just such an occasion. The Mongols had marched, plowing through European armies left and right clear to Vienna when the khan died and the whole thing was called off, never to be renewed.

Ogedei, Genghis' son. His death ended the invasion of Europe.

Other interruptions to the normal order of things occurred because of the Mongols too. The Crusades were called off for a short time so that the Muslims and Christians could unite against the common threat of the Mongol advance into the Holy Land. Life can be strange sometimes, but politics is the strangest of all.

Discuss power, government, and the ruling class with your kids.
- Why do people make war?
- Why do people want so badly to be in control of other people?
- What are the good and bad things about government?
- Do you want power? Why?
- What things are most important to make you happy and what does that have to do with this discussion?

MONGOLS – CAUCASUS – GASES & KINETIC THEORY- FUN WITH POETRY

☺ ☻ **EXPLORATION: The Yam**
The Mongol mail system, called the yam, was the best in the world until the advent of airplanes. There was a road system stretching all over the Empire, and all along the roads were station houses with couriers and fresh mounts. In some places dogsleds or boats were used as well. The letters or royal proclamations would travel from one courier to another in a long relay race across thousands of miles. This speed was essential to ruling an empire as large as the Mongols had created.

Have a relay race. First prepare a proclamation or personal letter on a scroll and pass it from one person to another along a pre-determined route. See how fast you can pass your message along.

When the khan died in Karakorum it took the messengers just six weeks to give the news to the military leaders near Vienna. On a world map look up how far it is from Karakorum to Vienna. How many miles did the news have to travel? How many miles a day did that mean it had to move? Remember too, that the distances you found were in a straight line, but distances on real land never can be flat and straight.

☺ ☻ **EXPLORATION: Tactics of Warfare**
Russian winters have defeated more enemies than Russian armies, but that does not include the Mongols. They reveled in harsh conditions . . . some sort of macho thing. They used the frozen rivers and lakes of Russia and other places as highways to make their attacks easier.

The Mongols reportedly reduced or annihilated the populations of every place they visited. Over the course of their conquests many hundreds of millions were killed. Sure makes keeping the locals in check much easier if there aren't any, but it also reduces the tax revenues. . . ah, the headaches of ruling.

The Mongols also used their cavalry and lancers to great effect. Their archers were mounted and only lightly armored. This made them light and maneuverable. They could decimate whole columns and dart out of the way before any counter attack could be mounted.

Their soldiers were very well trained. And virtually the whole population of adult males were in the army full time by law. Discipline was strict and punishments harsh, making for almost perfect obedience.

The Mongols also used machines of war, like trebuchets and

Fabulous Fact

The Mongols were originally shamanistic with some Buddhist influences via China. But they were very open and free with religion. People within the empire could worship any way they pleased. Some of the Mongol leaders in the west converted to the Islam of their captives. And so the power of the Islamic caliphates was destroyed, but not the religion itself, which continued to flourish in Persia and Central Asia.

Islamic Mongol descendents would later become the Mughal rulers of India. The fact that they are both Mongols and Muslims explains why they were much more tolerant of Hinduism, Buddhism, and minority religions in India than was traditional in Arabic Muslim states, where Islam was enforced with terribly harsh measures.

Fabulous Fact

Horses were extremely important to the Mongol way of life. They bred, loved, and cared for their horses with great attention.

MONGOLS – CAUCASUS – GASES & KINETIC THEORY- FUN WITH POETRY

On the Web

Watch this entertaining bit on the Mongols.

http://youtu.be/szxPar0BcMo

And this one focusing on the Mongols in Russia:

http://youtu.be/etmRI2_9Q_A

Fabulous Fact

In September of 1260 the Mamluks in the Holy Land beat the Mongols in battle at Ain Jalut, just a few miles north of Jerusalem. The Mongols had taken the cities of Homs and Damascus and were marching for Jerusalem when they were met by the Mamluks. The Mongols never did take the Holy Land and the Muslims remained in control of this much contested real estate.

Read more about the battle and the masterful planning and technique of the Mamluk leader.

catapults, on fortified towns. They brought engineers everywhere with their armies and could build machines on the spot in a few days or weeks.

Learn more about the Mongol war tactics and write a report on how they built such a huge empire with their military might. Discuss what you think of their tactics morally. Does might make right? Also, color the Mongol Warrior coloring sheet.

☺ ☻ **EXPLORATION: The Black Banner**
The traditional Mongol flag, and one that is in use today as well, is a circular banner made of horse tails. The white banner is used in times of peace and the black banner in times of war.

White horse hair banners of the Mongol Empire. Photo by Lkhmaa and shared under CC license on Wikimedia.

Make your own banner with a dowel stick, yarn, pipe cleaners, and 2 plastic lids.

Make a hole in the center of the plastic lids, just large enough for the dowel stick. Paint the plastic lids in metallic spray paint. Create a "horse tail" out of the yarn with a thick 3 foot long bunch, tied in the center with a rubber band. We kept the yarn in

Mongols – Caucasus – Gases & Kinetic Theory – Fun With Poetry

loops rather than cutting each piece. Next, stack your materials – first a lid, then your yarn horse tail, then the other lid, with the dowel poking through the center of each one. Spread the yarn evenly around the circle. Poke holes along the edge of the lids in 4 equidistant places and secure them together using pipe cleaners. Finally, give your flag a "haircut" by cutting it in equal lengths all around the edge of the lid.

Writer's Workshop

Write a persuasive essay entitled "Might versus Right."

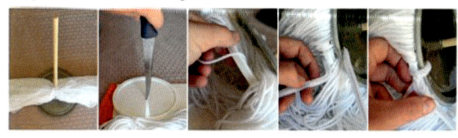

☺ ☺ ☺ **EXPLORATION: Disintegrating Empire**
It turned out that the Mongol Empire as a single political unit lasted less than fifty years. It was just too big to rule and Mongols, while very good at warfare, were terrible administrators. So it was divided into four administrative divisions. Very quickly these divisions began to play off one another, compete with one another, and sometimes go to war with one another. For the most part, they became completely separated by 1300. By 1365 the Mongol Empire was crumbling, and conquered states were taking back their land.

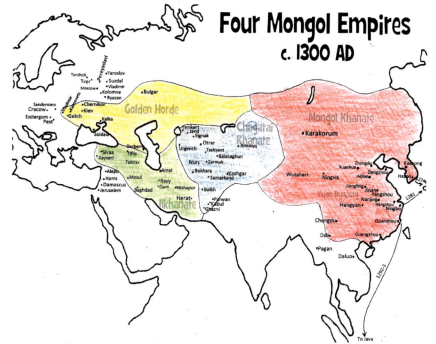

The map above can be found in the printables at the end of this unit. Color the map according to the divisions of the Mongol Empire.

Additional Layer

The city of Karakorum was built after Genghis won a battle on the site. At first it was just a town of Yurts. The Mongols did not build permanent cities. They were herdsmen, not farmers, and never had settled cities until they had an empire and needed a capital. Ogedei built a palace and city walls in 1235. Artisans from all over the Empire were brought to build and adorn the city. Temples, mosques, and churches of every major faith were built in the city and the centerpiece was a silver tree, crafted by a Paris silversmith.

The tree was made of pipes and dispensed beverages to the Khan's guests. In 1388 the city was destroyed by Ming invaders. Today it is a few scattered ruins.

Mongols – Caucasus – Gases & Kinetic Theory - Fun With Poetry

Additional Layer
Once the Mongols began to actually rule over vast lands they became diplomats, traders, and politicians. Envoys from as far away as Paris visited Karakorum. Mongol representatives visited Rome and other important cities of the west and established foreign relations. Trade between Europe and China flourished for the brief century that the Mongols controlled the trade routes.

Famous Folks
Rabban bar Sauma was a Christian Nestorian Mongol who became a diplomat for the court of the Khans in 1285. He made the long overland journey from China to Rome and Paris, meeting with the Pope and the French king, attempting to make treaties for the Mongol Empire. After he got back home he wrote an account of his journey, which happened at roughly the same time Marco Polo was traveling in the reverse direction from Europe to China.

☺ ☻ EXPLORATION: Kublai Khan
Kublai Khan was the emperor of China, but he was a Mongol. His grandfather, Genghis had begun the conquest of China many years earlier, but the Chinese far outnumbered and outclassed the Mongols militarily, culturally, and in every other way. So how did the Mongols end up ruling the Chinese?

Read this BBC article and see what you think:
http://www.bbc.co.uk/news/magazine-19850234

(There are no doubt links to articles or sites that are not appropriate for children on this page, though the article itself is innocuous. Supervise your kids.)

Learn more about Kublai Khan. Write a report on him. Especially focus on what you think made him a successful ruler. You can also combine the poetry and history sections of this unit by reading and analyzing the poem about Kublai Khan from the printables at the end of the unit.

☺ ☻ EXPLORATION: Mongolian Helmet
Make a Mongol helmet out of a bleach bottle and cardboard. The conical Mongolian helmet was made of metal, usually iron. Then three large leather flaps, studded with metal rivets were attached around the rim, two over the ears, and one at the back of the head to protect the neck.

Make your own out of a bleach bottle, with the bottom cut off and three wide flaps of cardboard, stapled to the bottom of the bottle. Spray paint the bottle in a metallic color and the flaps in brown.

An actual Mongol helmet. A tail of horsehair probably flowed from the top of the point in the center of the helmet.

MONGOLS – CAUCASUS – GASES & KINETIC THEORY- FUN WITH POETRY

GEOGRAPHY: CAUCASUS

The countries of Georgia, Armenia, and Azerbaijan are all found in the south Caucasus Mountains, right on the border between the geographical regions of Europe and Asia. The whole region is generally mountainous, but also contains temperate rainforests, marshlands, grassy plains, and forests. The region has varied climates because of the way the mountains divert the cool weather from the north. There are areas with cool summers and snowy, wet winters and areas with warmer sub-tropical climates.

GEORGIA

Anciently this part of the world was called Iberia. The Spanish peninsula is also called Iberia, but the two are not connected (as far as we know). The land was overrun by Alexander the Great, the Romans, the Huns, the Turks, the Mongols, the Persians, and the Russians. The kings intermittently struggled for freedom and paid tribute for peace. Anciently the people practiced Zoroastrianism. In the first century AD they adopted Christianity (it was adopted as the state religion in 321 or thereabouts) and have been a Christian nation ever since. In 1821 Georgia declared independence from Russia during the general revolutions of the period. They were independent until 1921 when the Red Army of Russia reconquered them. Under the Soviets, more than 200,000 Georgians were killed in cultural "purges." Through most of the 20th century Georgia was under communist rule and the harsh economic policies and state-owned economy made a thriving and

Additional Layer

The southern part of Russia, including the federal states of Dagestan, Chechnya, Ossetia, and others, is also in the Caucasus region and the people there have cultures very different from the mainstream Moscow culture.

Many of these people wanted independence when the rest of the USSR was falling apart in the early 1990's. But Russia resisted and the international community did not insist. Today there is much political tension in the area. Most terrorist attacks on Russian targets originate in Chechnya or Dagestan.

Additional Layer

The whole Caucases region is politically unstable. There are nations within Georgia that also desire independence and South Ossetia and Abkhazia within Georgia function almost completely independently. But almost no one in the international community recognizes them as independent states.

Mongols – Caucasus – Gases & Kinetic Theory – Fun With Poetry

Fabulous Fact
The U.S. has a program called "Train and Equip" to help Georgia's armed forces come up to speed.

Georgian troops have been active in Afghanistan in the War on Terror.

Additional Layer
Georgian tradition states that the people of their region are descended directly from Japheth, son of the famous Noah of the Bible. According to tradition, all of Europe descends from Japheth, while Africa descends from Ham and Asia descends from Shem.

Additional Layer
The name Azerbaijan means "guardians of fire" and goes way back to when Zoroastrianism was the religion of the area.

blatantly corrupt shadow economy very successful. The people of Georgia were relatively well-to-do since they flaunted the laws and carried on commerce under a black market. In 1991 Georgia re-declared its independence from Russia and, after a time, other nations recognized the independence as well. But independence did not bring peace. Georgia has been riddled with coups, assassinations, corruption, mafia activity, additional invasions and interference from Russia, and more suffering than its people deserve. Their government is now organized as a republic, with multiple political parties and a written constitution. Economically they are mostly capitalist.

Old part of Tbilisi, the capital of Georgia.

ARMENIA

Like Georgia, Armenia was a former Soviet satellite country. They have an ancient history and cultural heritage as well. They too adopted Christianity as the state religion very early in 301 AD. The country has been called Armenia from the time of the Greeks and before that it was called Ararat. Like Georgia, Armenia has been overrun by various peoples again and again. It lies directly between two seas and at the crossroads between many great civilizations. Twice during the Ottoman rule the Armenians were massacred by the state. First, in 1894, in the Hamidian Massacres somewhere between 80,000 and 300,000 people were killed. Then, in 1915, the Armenian Genocide, at the hands of their own Ottoman government, killed around 600,000 people.

Mongols – Caucasus – Gases & Kinetic Theory- Fun With Poetry

Later Russia peacefully annexed Armenia through treaty and a short period of peace ensued, allowing Armenia time to recover just in time for the reign of terror inflicted by Joseph Stalin during the Great Purge when many thousands more Armenians were killed. Armenia finally gained its independence in 1991. Economic and political strife followed this great upheaval as the country struggled to get back on its feet. They have emerged as a republic with separation of powers, a written constitution, and a multi-party system. Their economy is mostly capitalist.

Lake Sevan in Armenia, photo by Vigan Hakaverdyan, CC license

AZERBAIJAN

Azerbaijan is quite different from Armenia and Georgia. Its people are Turkic and Muslim. They were Zoroastrians first, then converted to Christianity early like Armenia and Georgia. In the Middle Ages the local population was overrun by Turks from the east and the local people were killed, pushed out or assimilated for the most part, though there are a few rural pockets of the old people there still. The Turks adopted Islam. Over the years the nation was ruled by first one, and then another foreign empire, culminating with the Russians in the 20th century. Azerbaijan regained independence from Russia in 1991.

Azerbaijan is also unique in the Muslim world in having a democratic, secular government. Before the invasion by Vladimir Lenin's forces, the nation of Azerbaijan had two brief years to govern themselves. In that time they extended universal suffrage to all adults and gave women equal political status with men.

Additional Layer

The fortress of Keselo with its thirteen towers was built in the 1230's when the Mongols were invading. The people would leave their villages and rush into the towers for protection when they heard the armies were on their way.

Photo by Lidia Ilona, CC

Today only five of the towers stand.

You can see more pictures of the towers and the valleys they stand in here: http://youtu.be/pDuZ56Z3hAA

On the Web

Watch this dance from the Georgian National Ballet. You'll hear some traditional Georgian instruments too, including a flute, stringed instruments, and the drums.

http://youtu.be/AQOKBdnBLzc

Then watch these kids perform more traditional dances:
http://youtu.be/uWJiXAfPEcI

Mongols – Caucasus – Gases & Kinetic Theory – Fun With Poetry

Additional Layer

This is the castle of Ananuri in Georgia.

In 1739 the Dukes of Ananuri were attacked by a rival dukedom, the castle burned, and the entire family killed. A few years later the peasants rose up against the usurper duke and killed him and his family, desiring instead to be ruled directly by the king and have no duke.

Learn more about the fortress here: http://youtu.be/JIGVz8V79Mg

Additional Layer

Georgia was having fits trying to get tax compliance and enough money to run the government until they introduced a hugely simplified flat tax to replace the former tax. Their revenues have increased four fold and a previous budget deficit has turned into a budget surplus, allowing the country to pay off some of its debts.

They also set up a democratic republic and were working on a constitution. When the country finally regained independence seventy years later they embraced the ideals of those two brief years and set up a secular republic once again. But the country still has had problems with disputed territories claimed by Armenia and they are not as economically free as most republics. Azerbaijan is also one of the few Muslim countries that has contributed troops to the War on Terror in Iraq and Afghanistan.

☺ ☺ ☺ EXPLORATION: Map

Color a map of Georgia, Armenia, and Azerbaijan. You can find a blank outline map at the end of this unit. Use a student atlas. Label each of the countries. Draw in the mountain ranges. Label the mountain ranges. Label the capital cities. Label the Black Sea and the Caspian Sea. Find the Caucasus on a globe or world map.

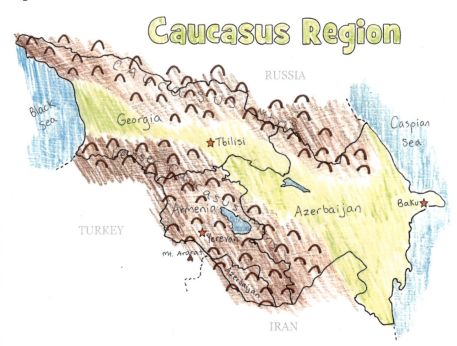

☺ ☺ ☺ EXPLORATION: Biography

Learn about one of these famous Georgians and write a report:
- King David Agmashenebeli (the Builder)
- Queen Tamar
- King George the Brilliant
- Joseph Stalin
- Ilia Chavchavadze
- Akaki Tsereteli
- Zviad Gamsakhurdia

Mongols – Caucasus – Gases & Kinetic Theory – Fun With Poetry

☺ ☻ **EXPLORATION: Flag**
Georgia is called "Georgia" because of their reverence for St. George, the dragonslayer, an early Christian hero and martyr. The flag of Georgia features the cross of St. George. Make a Georgian flag. Use the coloring sheet from the end of this unit.

Fabulous Fact

Much of Georgia is temperate pine forests and mountains, but the coast on the Black Sea is definitely sub-tropical as you see in the picture above.

☺ ☻ **EXPLORATION: Spelunking**
The deepest known cave is Krubera Cave in Georgia. It is in the Arabika Massif on the northwestern edge of the Black Sea. A massif is a distinct section of a continental plate. The whole area is riddled with karst caves and hot springs. The cave reaches at least 2,191 meters deep. That is deeper than the Grand Canyon in the United States. Make a chart or graph comparing some of the deepest places on earth. Include Krubera Cave. Learn more about the geology of the Caucasus Mountains.

☺ ☻ ☻ **EXPLORATION: Kinkali**
A traditional food from eastern Georgia is Kinkali, a meat or cheese filled dumpling.

    Dough:
    6 cups flour
    2 ½ tsp. salt
    3 cups warm water

Combine the flour and salt and stir in the water, kneading the dough.
    Filling:
    1 ½ lbs. ground beef or pork, uncooked
    1 tsp. ground black pepper

Additional Layer

As a former Soviet state in recovery, Georgian people are still below western European people in terms of wealth, but their outlook is good. They have instituted many free market practices and unemployment is dropping as wages are rising. Russia has declared economic warfare on Georgia including raising the price of oil sales to Georgia and banning Georgian imports.

Georgia produces wine, copper, gold, silver, iron, and other agricultural products. Tourism is also a major source of income for the beautiful little country in the Caucasus.

Examine these countries and determine what principles make nations wealthy.

MONGOLS – CAUCASUS – GASES & KINETIC THEORY - FUN WITH POETRY

Additional Layer
In 2008 Georgia went to war with South Ossetia, one of its provinces. South Ossetia wanted to secede and Georgia didn't want it to. Russia, ironically, since it won't let any of its states go free, came into the conflict on the side of the South Ossetians. South Ossetia, now occupied by Soviet troops, is ruling itself under protest by Georgia, which claims the province is not free, but merely occupied by the Russians. The international community tends to agree and South Ossetia is still officially part of Georgia.

2 tsp. salt
2 small onions, grated
1 ½ cups water

Mix all ingredients in a large bowl.

Bring a large pot of water to a boil. Take small balls of dough and roll out thinly to an 8" diameter, similar to the size of a tortilla. You can make them smaller if you'd like so they are easier to handle, but don't make them any larger. Place a spoonful of filling into the center of the dough. Pull the edges of the dough up around the filling and pleat the edges together, pressing to seal. Set the waiting dumplings on a well floured counter top to wait. Boil the dumplings, about 15 at a time, or as many as fit into your pot, for about ten minutes.

The filling will be very juicy and messy, so eat with care. Most people do not eat the pleated tops of the dumplings as they tend to get tough. The dumplings are usually eaten plain or with extra pepper for seasoning.

Additional Layer

Noah's "mountains of Ararat" are located in the Armenian highlands by tradition. The ancient Kingdom of Armenia was called Ararat. Though the actual mountain suspected of being the resting place of the ark is now just inside the border of Turkey. Armenians claim to be descended from a great grandson of Noah who they deem their patriarch.

☺ ☻ ☺ **EXPLORATION: Armenian Language**
Armenia has its own unique alphabet and language. Most Armenians also speak Russian and more and more are learning English as it is the lingua franca of the business world and politics in Europe.

The Armenian saint, Mesrop Mashtots, invented the alphabet for the Armenian language in 405 AD so the previously illiterate people could read the Bible in their own language.

Mongols – Caucasus – Gases & Kinetic Theory - Fun With Poetry

To see what the characters of the alphabet look like go to an online text translator: http://www.translator.am/en/translate.html. Type in whatever you like and it will be translated into Armenian characters. By moving your mouse over the words you can see the phonetic pronunciation.

😊 😊 EXPLORATION: Azerbaijan Flora and Fauna

Azerbaijan has an extremely varied and interesting natural world since it has such varied landscapes, and its mountains protect it from the cold northern weather patterns. Due to the Caspian and Black seas it does get plenty of moisture. Learn more about the plants and animals of Azerbaijan and make a diorama showing some of them off.

First paint the insides of a shoe box to show the background and then add in animals and plants made of paper and glued into the box.

Explain your diorama to a group.

😊 😊 😊 EXPLORATION: Religion

Make a graph showing the people of different faiths in Azerbaijan. (numbers are estimates)

    Total number of people in the country = 9,047,000
    Non-religious (mostly of Muslim heritage) = 4,523,500
    Practicing Islamic = 3,890,210
    Christian = 361,880
    Other = 162,800
    Zoroastrian = 2000

😊 EXPLORATION: Fire Temple of Baku

The Fire Temple of Baku is an ancient temple found in Azerbaijan.

It is built above fields of natural gas and often spontaneous fires would alight through vents in the rock. Some think it was a Zoroastrian site

Additional Layer
Half of the world's mud volcanoes are in Azerbaijan. Learn more about mud volcanoes.

Fabulous Fact
In 1918 Armenians and Russian Bolsheviks murdered hundreds of Azerbaijani people including women and children. Their bodies were thrown into several wells and rediscovered in 2007 during the construction of a stadium.

This part of the world has been the scene of unrest for thousands of years, resulting in the deaths of millions of civilians as well as soldiers.

Additional Layer
Countries that do not have a declared national religion are considered secular governments. Azerbaijan is one of the few nations with a Muslim majority that also has a secular government. Find out more about Azerbaijan's government and that of neighboring Iran. Compare the two. What conclusions do you come to? Think it through carefully. Are the comparisons because of the Muslim religion or something else?

Mongols – Caucasus – Gases & Kinetic Theory - Fun With Poetry

since they use fire in their worship. Others believe it to be a Hindu site as they also use fire. Today it is a museum and tourist site.

Learn more about it and create a poster with pictures and facts about the site.

😊 🟢 EXPLORATION: Celebrate Nowruz

Nowruz means "new light" in Persian and has been celebrated by the people of Azerbaijan since before Islam, before Christianity, and originating with Zoroastrianism. It is a truly ancient celebration. It occurs during the vernal equinox (March 20th or 21st), celebrating the return of spring and the light part of the year. It is the beginning of the new year in Azerbaijan and other nations once controlled by the Persian Empire.

Celebrations begin with a spring house cleaning, a purchase of new clothes for the year, and filling the house with spring flowers. The evening before they visit the graves of loved ones lost. On the day of Nowruz they put on their new clothes and have a gift exchange. Then they go visiting their relatives and friends over the subsequent 12 days and are visited in return. The last night they make big bonfires in the streets and party. People jump over small fires to symbolize the fire burning away all the bad and to give them good luck for the new year. Children go door to door asking for candy. On the thirteenth day they go picnicking out of doors. The many traditions associated with the holiday have religious and symbolic significance.

Write your congressman and ask for Nowruz to be made a U.S. national holiday. Well, not really, but it sure sounds fun, doesn't it? You *can* get the house all cleaned up, put on some nice clothes, set the table pretty, and try some Azerbaijani dishes for dinner. Afterward go out and have a fire in the backyard or at least light some candles.

The whole holiday is very involved and interesting. Read more about it if you get the chance.

Additional Layer

Azerbaijan is very rich in oil and is the main reason the Bolsheviks invaded and took over the Caucasus region. It is also the main reason the Nazis pushed toward the Caucasus during WWII, though they never made it that far.

Oil pump near Baku, photo by Gulustan

Today the oil fields are helping Azerbaijan recover economically from communism.

On the Web

Azerbaijan has its own unique fairy tales like other lands on Earth. Meet Jirtdan, a heroic tiny child who uses his mind rather than his muscles:

http://azer.com/aiweb/categories/magazine/43_folder/43_articles/43_children.html

MONGOLS – CAUCASUS – GASES & KINETIC THEORY- FUN WITH POETRY

CHEMISTRY: GASES & KINETIC THEORY

As we have learned, everything around us is made of tiny molecules, which are made of atoms. All of these atoms are constantly moving, even in things that look like they are pretty firm and solid. Molecules in a solid just vibrate against one another. The colder something gets the less the molecules move. If you could cool something to absolute zero, only then would the molecules and atoms stop moving. In liquids the molecules move more than in solids, and in gases they move even more. The warmer a substance gets, the faster and more wildly it moves. This change in movement is, in fact, why substances change from solid to liquid to gas. The word "kinetic" means movement and so when we speak of "Kinetic Theory" we mean the idea that everything moves all the time.

On the Web
This little video is a great introduction to kinetic theory for younger kids.

http://youtu.be/_TsqDNhFG1Y

Fabulous Fact
Isaac Newton thought that gases held pressure against the edges of their containers through static repulsion between the molecules.

Modern theory says that, no, actually molecules are moving, like really, really fast, and it is the collisions against the edge of the container that keep a balloon blown up.

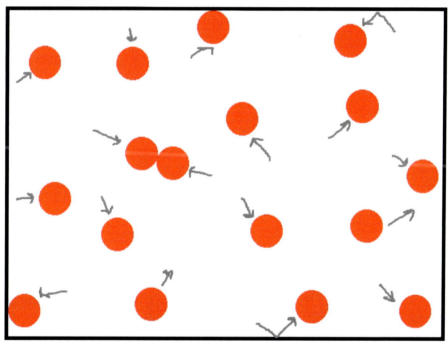

Because molecules in a gas are moving all the time, they will diffuse, or spread out to fill their container. Each molecule wants as much space as possible, and filling the container maximizes their space. If you heat a closed container of gas, you may cause it to explode as the molecules move faster and faster. Temperature and volume of a gas are very closely related as we will see in the experiments below.

☺ ☺ ☺ **EXPLORATION: Popcorn Matter Demonstration**
1. Put a handful of popcorn kernels and 1 cube of melted

Famous Folks
Daniel Bernoulli was the first to theorize that it was the movement of gas molecules that accounted for their properties.

Mongols – Caucasus – Gases & Kinetic Theory – Fun With Poetry

Fabulous Fact
Did you know that Benjamin Franklin did experiments on refrigeration while he was an ambassador for the Colony of Pennsylvania in Great Britain in the 1750's? He worked with Cambridge University professor John Hadley.

On the Web
This 1950's film from the U.S. government explains refrigeration in twenty minutes.
http://youtu.be/b527al9D_rY

Additional Layer
They say that refrigeration has saved more lives than all the modern medical knowledge combined. Research the history of food preservation and refrigeration in particular. What do you think?

Famous Folks
The relationship between temperature and the volume of a gas was discovered by Jacques Charles in 1787.

Charles' Law says that temperature and volume are directly proportional. If the temperature is cut in half, then the volume is also cut in half.

---

butter into a sauce pan. Place the pan into the fridge to make the butter solidify around the popcorn kernels.
2. Explain the principle that as molecules heat they move more and expand, turning from solids to liquids to gases. At each stage they get further apart and move more and more.
3. Put the pan of butter and popcorn kernels on the stove, showing how they are solid and cool.
4. Turn the heat on the stove to medium.
5. Watch as the kernels and butter heat up, turning to a liquid which can be swirled around the pan. It is now too hot to touch.
6. Leave the lid off the pan as popcorn kernels begin to pop around the room. They have now heated up so much that they have become a "gas," with the molecules moving very fast and spreading much further apart to diffuse over the whole room.
7. Make a new batch or have some pre-prepared popcorn for the kids to eat while you discuss more about kinetic theory.

Be sure the kids understand that this an object lesson, the popcorn kernels are not actually a gas. You should follow it up with some actual experiments using the real thing.

☺ ☺ EXPLORATION: Refrigeration
Things like refrigerators and air conditioners work on the principle of expanding gases. Do some research to learn how they work and draw a diagram explaining the process.

☺ ☺ EXPERIMENT: Freezing a balloon
1. Blow up a balloon, tie it off.
2. Weigh it. You will need a sensitive scale, like a kitchen food scale. The bathroom scale won't be accurate enough. If you don't have such a scale, skip weighing it.
3. Put the balloon in the freezer.
4. Check it after ten minutes.
5. Weigh it again.

Mongols – Caucasus – Gases & Kinetic Theory - Fun With Poetry

The balloon shrinks in the cold air of the freezer, because the molecules move slower and take up less space. But it should weigh the same before and after.

🙂 🙂 🙂 EXPERIMENT: Brownian Motion
1. Fill a glass or small dish with water
2. Let it sit for five minutes for the water to stop flowing.
3. Sprinkle some pollen grains on the surface of the water. Either get the pollen grains from your yard or purchase flowers with pollen stocks.
4. Observe the pollen grains very carefully.

You will see the pollen grains move around in a random manner, jerking to and fro on the surface of the water. This is exactly what scientist Robert Brown observed. This sort of random motion became known as Brownian motion. Why do you think the pollen grains move this way? Robert Brown didn't ever figure it out. Seventy years later Albert Einstein figured out the cause of Brownian motion using kinetic theory. Find some dust motes in a beam of sunlight in a draft free room and see if they behave similarly.

🙂 🙂 EXPERIMENT: Expanding Liquids
Put a thermometer (non-electric) in a glass of ice water. Observe how the liquid inside the gauge moves down the tube of the thermometer. Now put the thermometer into a glass of boiling water. Observe the liquid in the thermometer again. Why does the liquid move up and down? The answer is that when liquids warm up they expand because of the molecules moving faster.

> **Famous Folks**
> Learn more about one of the scientists who studied kinetic theory and the laws of gases: Robert Boyle, Ludwig Boltzman, Robert Brown, Albert Einstein, Amedo Avagadro, Joseph Louis Guy-Lussac, or Jacques Charles.

> **On the Web**
> Your high schooler can learn about gases and their properties with Khan Academy.
> https://www.khanacademy.org/science/chemistry/ideal-gas-laws

> **On the Web**
> NASA has a page on kinetic theory along with age appropriate experiments to try with your kids.
> http://www.grc.nasa.gov/WWW/k-12/airplane/kinth.html

> **Fabulous Fact**
> Diffusion is the random motion of stuff that causes the stuff to be distributed equally throughout a system. Diffusion is a concept in science, but also in sociology (the diffusion of ideas) and finance (the diffusion of price values), plus other fields.

Mongols – Caucasus – Gases & Kinetic Theory - Fun With Poetry

Fabulous Fact

Human eyes don't get enough oxygen through the blood stream because there are relatively few blood vessels in the eye. So, weirdly, oxygen is absorbed through the cornea by diffusion from the atmosphere.

On the Web

Watch this video about Graham's Law, which explains the diffusion speeds of gases.

http://youtu.be/g6Quuo Ts2Oo

For High Schoolers

Avogadro's Law says that if you have a certain mass of gas molecules, then the volume of the gas will be proportional to the moles of the gas as long as the temperature and pressure are constant. Moles means the amount of stuff. This leads to the ideal gas law, which you can learn about at Khan Academy, link on the previous page, or in Chapter 8 of *Chemistry: A Self-Teaching Guide* by Houk.

☺ ☺ EXPERIMENT: Diffusion In A Liquid

1. Prepare two glasses of water – one cold and one hot.
2. Let them sit for five minutes to allow the water to stop moving.
3. At the same time drop a few drops of food coloring into each glass. No stirring.
4. Observe how the food coloring spreads in the water.

Before you drop the food coloring in have the kids make up a hypothesis about what they think will happen. You can have them write it out on an experiment form or you can just state the hypothesis orally.

The warmer water causes the food coloring to diffuse more rapidly since the molecules of water are moving faster. But after a time both glasses will be uniformly colored with the coloring. You can time how long it takes the food coloring to be completely diffused in each glass. Notice that the food coloring expands to fill every part of the container, making each molecule as far apart as possible.

☺ ☺ EXPLORATION: Diffusion In A Gas

Before you start the lesson on kinetic theory put a pan of brownies or cookies in to bake. Hopefully the kids will notice the smell and become curious. Ask them why they can smell brownies that are clear across the room, or the house, and inside an oven. The scent of the brownies diffuses through the house and fills the whole space. This is diffusion through a gas.

MONGOLS – CAUCASUS – GASES & KINETIC THEORY- FUN WITH POETRY

☺ ☻ EXPERIMENT: Heat and Pressure

Besides heat having an effect on a gas, pressure also changes how a gas behaves. The air inside a bicycle pump is contained in a cylinder and forced through a small tube. This increases the pressure each time the handle is pumped. What effect does pressure have on a gas? Find out by pumping the bicycle pump a dozen times rapidly. Feel the air cylinder of the pump. It should heat up. As the pressure increases, the gas molecules must move faster and as they move faster they give off energy as heat, heating the bicycle pump.

☺ ☻ ☻ EXPERIMENT: Boyle's Law

1. Set a pot of water on the stove and turn the heat up to high.
2. Watch the bubbles as they form on the bottom of the pan. The bubbles are water vapor, water changed to a gas by the heat. They form on the bottom of the pan, because that is where the heat is.
3. Observe the size of the bubbles at the bottom of the pan and how they change as they rise through the water. You should be able to see them grow larger.

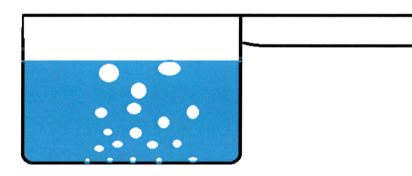

Why do the bubbles get larger as they near the surface of the water? Pressure means the force pushing in or down on an object. If the force is greater, we say there is greater pressure. Where in the water is the largest amount of pressure? As the bubble moves up through the water the pressure on it decreases and the bubble can expand, each molecule taking up more space, until it bursts out of the water and diffuses through the air in the room. The principles regarding expansion of gases in a liquid are called Boyle's Law. If the pressure of a gas is greater, then the volume of the gas is less.

☻ ☻ EXPLORATION: Expansion Of A Solid

Though solids do not expand as much or as quickly as liquids and gases, they do expand. When bridges are built, space is left between the steel girders, so when the steel expands in the

---

Famous Folks

Amateur scientist, Richard Townley was the one who actually discovered Boyle's Law. He, along with Henry Power, were in correspondence with Robert Boyle who proved that Townley's theory about gases was correct. Boyle published the results and the law was named after him.

On the Web

Visit NASA's animated gas lab to learn more about the properties of gases.

http://www.grc.nasa.gov/WWW/k-12/airplane/Animation/frglab.html

Memorization Station

Memorize the definitions of these gas laws and concepts:

Kinetic Theory

Brownian Motion

Charles' Law

Gay-Lussac's Law

Avogadro's Law

Boyle's Law

Mongols – Caucasus – Gases & Kinetic Theory – Fun With Poetry

Additional Layer

Learn about the Eiffel tower.

summer heat the bridge doesn't break. The Eiffel Tower grows three inches every summer because of expansion. Railway lines include gaps between the rails to allow for expansion in the summer heat. If you build a deck on your house, you have to leave small gaps between the boards to allow for expansion. Often wooden houses creak at night as they cool down in the night air. Heated glass will crack and break if it cools too quickly because uneven cooling will cause some parts to contract more quickly than others. Spark plugs are made of ceramic designed with very small expansion rates. The spark plug body must be non-conducting and also able to withstand repeated massive temperature fluctuations. Spark plugs are a marvel of human ingenuity. Learn more about one of these solid expansions or find an example on your own. Write a report with diagrams to explain what expansion occurs and how people allow for the expansion in engineering and technology.

☺ ☺ ☺ **EXPERIMENT: Hot Air Balloon**

Make a hot air balloon out of tissue paper to show how heated gases are lighter because they have expanded. Make panels of tissue paper in football shapes. Glue each panel together and place a hoop, like the rim of a margarine lid, an embroidery hoop, or even a cardboard ring around the bottom rim. Heat the air inside the balloon with a hair dryer to make it rise into the air. Explain why the balloon rises with heat. What does this have to do with kinetic theory and the behavior of gases?

On the Web

An explosion is rapid diffusion of gases when a great number of gas molecules are produced in a very short time. Diffusion is not always slow and quiet.

Make a PVC rocket launcher and foam rocket powered by hairspray. To see this in action:

www.layers-of-learning.com/pvc-rocket/

Additional Layer

Learn about the history of hot air balloons.

The Arts: Fun With Poetry

Poetry is different from prose; it is writing that concisely and intensely expresses emotions and ideas. Often it is written in a particular form or style, though this doesn't have to be so. When people are first exploring how to write poems, it can be helpful to have specific formats or very specific assignments to help them as they explore playing with words without the confinement of the conventions and rules of normal prose. As kids write more and more poetry, fewer forms and expectations can be put in place. This unit includes explorations to help beginning poets have fun with poetry in a directed way. Read as many fun and interesting poems as possible, and then enjoy writing and playing with words. An artist uses paint; a poet uses words.

Teaching Tip
Sometimes writing poetry feels stressful to kids, but it should really be the opposite. Poets get to throw out conventions. Capitals and punctuation and complete sentences don't matter. All the typical writing rules go out the door and you get to just play with words. Poems are like potato chips; you can't eat just one. Any exploration in this unit could be done over and over again with new words and in new ways. Write as many as you like. Be surprising. Have fun.

Karen

Teaching Tip
Having a dictionary and a thesaurus nearby during a poetry unit is absolutely essential. I also like to use online rhyming dictionaries sometimes.

☺ ☺ ☺ EXPLORATION: Doors Galore
Poets use words concisely. Complete sentences and structure are less important than the meaning and description behind the words. Practice writing concisely with this activity.

Imagine a door. It could be any kind of door you wish – a castle door, a hospital door, a car door, a factory door, a spaceship door, a haunted mansion door, any door you wish. Draw the door. Now take your drawing and write a description of what is behind the door in a dozen words or less. Don't bother to use small

Mongols – Caucasus – Gases & Kinetic Theory – Fun With Poetry

Teaching Tip

It can help a lot of kids to actually write out a descriptive paragraph first. Kids usually have more practice writing whole paragraphs, so this is easier. Then you can help them turn their paragraph into a poem by removing all the unnecessary words.

We've spent so much time drilling punctuation and grammar in (necessarily) that it's really hard to let go of that and wrap your head around the sparing use of words that is poetry.

This paragraph:

I like autumn because the air smells crisp and the grass is covered with frost in the morning. I also get to play soccer again.

Becomes this:

Crisp air
Frosty blades of grass
Soccer field, I'll be there
kick, run, and pass

Teaching Tip

Sometimes kids believe that poetry = rhyming. Rhyming is fun, but not essential. Tell them that for every rhyming poem they write, they owe you one that doesn't rhyme.

words like "a" or "the." Don't bother to use complete sentences. Just use the most important words to tell what awaits behind the door in the shortest way possible.

☺ ☺ ☺ EXPLORATION: Dictionary Poems

Start by choosing one of these words that you will write a poem about:

- love
- hatred
- prejudice
- play
- joy
- nature
- knowledge
- crime
- pollution
- friendship
- fame

Now get out a dictionary and look up your word. Make note of descriptive words that tell vividly about the word you chose. Now play with and rearrange the words in poetic form. Here is an example of a dictionary poem:

Mongols – Caucasus – Gases & Kinetic Theory – Fun With Poetry

<u>Prejudice</u>

Unkind,
Unreasonable,
BIAS.
A dislike of people
for no good reason
before you even know them.

Have someone read your poem without revealing the title and see if they can pinpoint your focus word without being told.

☺ ☺ ☺ **EXPLORATION: Colors in Me**
Sometimes when we write poems it helps to begin with a word bank of sorts. We can brainstorm descriptions and interesting language and then use our ideas as we write poems. Here is a way that you can begin a word bank using colors.

Close your eyes. Imagine that you are in a dark room. A color will come into the room and go right through you. As it goes through your body you will feel varying degrees of hot or cold and you will describe it out loud. You might feel other things too, emotions like loneliness, fear, happiness, or elation. You can also use your other senses as you imagine these experiences. Write down the descriptions that come to you in your word bank.

Here are some color descriptions to start from:

Feel orange as it comes into the room. Your blood is turning orange. Your heart is pumping orange. Your whole body is orange. How do you feel?

Feel purple as it comes into the room. It is coming in like a wave and filling the whole room from top to bottom and you are smack dab in the middle. How do you feel?

Feel yellow as it comes into the room. It's falling through the sky, soaking everything, and turning it yellow too. Bit by bit, you and everything in the room is consumed with yellow. How do you feel?

Feel black as it comes into the room. Blackness is everywhere all at once, and everything else disappears. You try to adjust your eyes, but the blackness has enveloped you and become you. How do you feel?

Additional Layer

Spot the descriptions in poems you are reading. Here's one to practice on:

The cow
Coming
Across the grass
Moves
Like a mountain
Toward us;
Her hipbones
Jut
Like sharp peaks
Of stone,
Her hoofs
Thump
Like dropped
Rocks:
Almost
Too late
She stops.

-Valerie Worth

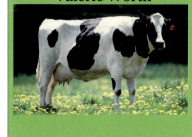

Additional Layer

Don't forget to read poetry too. Have you tried these poets:

Kenn Nesbitt

Jon Scieszka

Marilyn Singer

Barry Louis Polisar

Allan Ahlberg

Roald Dahl

MONGOLS – CAUCASUS – GASES & KINETIC THEORY - FUN WITH POETRY

Memorization Station

<u>Eletelephony</u>

Once there was an elephant,

Who tried to use the telephant -

No! No! I mean an elephone

Who tried to use the telephone -

Dear me! I am not certain quite

That even now I've got it right.

Howe'er it was, he got his trunk

Entangled in the telephunk;

The more he tried to get it free,

The louder buzzed the telephee -

I fear I'd better drop the song

Of elephop and telephong!

 -Laura E. Richards

Fabulous Fact

Not all rhyme schemes use perfect rhymes. Sometimes poets use slant rhymes, which are close, but not quite rhymes. For example, "rocket" and "pocket" rhyme, but "rocket" and "chocolate" are slant rhymes.

Keep adding on more colors and writing down the ideas and descriptions as you go.

Examples:
- It's as cold as ice water trickling down my back.
- It's hot like swimming through the lava of a volcano.
- It is as lonely as a gray gull scanning the empty sky.
- It shines as bright as the sun that makes me squint and shy away from its rays.
- It's like a siren, making me cover my ears!
- It tastes like vinegar and I want to spit it out!

Discuss how any experience can be described this way. If we are sitting on a bridge overlooking a river or driving in busy traffic, we can tell about our experience in a way that others will experience and feel what we do. Practice this and write down your ideas in your writer's notebook.

😊 😊 😊 EXPLORATION: "Like What" Lists

You can describe any object or feeling using a "Like What" list. This is another way to make a word bank or get the creative poetry juices flowing. You will choose an object or an emotion and then describe it using a variety of ways like color, temperature, sound, taste, smell, look, texture, and movement. The best way to teach this is just to show an example:

Anger can be . . .
red like tomato sauce boiling over on Mom's stove
gray like a mean storm cloud crashing through the sky
cold like icicles jutting off the roof
cold like a friend who is acting like she hates you
stinky like a skunk under the back deck
gross like a rotten egg
like a cobra with venom coursing through my brain
jolting as ocean waves thrashing the shore

Now try your own. Once you start describing things in new ways like these, they'll come to you more and more easily.

😊 😊 EXPLORATION: Telephone Syllables

One fun trick poets use is playing with syllables. In this kind of poem there is only one rule: you can only use as many syllables as your phone number says.

Write your phone number vertically down the side of your paper. Now fill in each line only using that many syllables. Here's one:

Mongols – Caucasus – Gases & Kinetic Theory – Fun With Poetry

5 Nature is my friend.
5 The outdoors call me.
5 I ride, run, jump, swing.
8 Come play outside with me today
0
7 Trees, clouds, sunshine, flowers, grass.
3 Happy day!

☺ **EXPLORATION: Rhyming**
Not all poems rhyme, but rhyme is certainly a fun element that can be a part of poetry. Rhyme schemes are labeled using letters. Any time the letter repeats means that is a line that must rhyme with its matching letter. Practice rhyming by finishing these poems that use various rhyme schemes:

ABCB rhyme scheme means that the 2nd and 4th lines are the only ones that need to rhyme. See how the B's match, so those are the lines that must rhyme?

> Each time I play baseball
> I hit a foul ball
> I think that just maybe
> _____.

ABAB means that the 1st and 3rd lines must rhyme along with the 2nd and 4th.

> I like to picnic in the park.
> I take a basket of food.
> All around me the dogs bark.
> _____.

AAAA means every line must rhyme.

> I want to go to outer space.
> I want to get out of this place!
> I'm going to pack my big suitcase.
> _____.

ABCB is one of the most common and easiest to do; here's one more:

> I dreamed I was riding a zebra
> He had pink hair on his head
> But when I woke up in the morning
> _____.

Additional Layer

This is a great place to introduce *denotation* and *connotation*.

Denotation is the literal dictionary definition of a word. Connotation is the feelings invoked by that word.

A house is a dwelling place. But "home" means safety, comfort, security, peace, and love.

Other words with strong connotations:

rain, winter, sunshine, princess, America, soldier, peace, drizzle, fog, lightning, skunk . . .

Read The Rainy Day by Longfellow and look for the words with strong connotations.

Using the right words with connotations in your poems will make them stronger.

Couplets

A couplet is a two line little rhyme. It could be part of a larger poem, a poem that stands on its own, or even a rhyme in the middle of otherwise ordinary prose.

This couplet is by Alexander Pope:

A little learning is a dangerous thing;/Drink deep, or taste not the Pierian spring.

Mongols – Caucasus – Gases & Kinetic Theory - Fun With Poetry

Tercets

A tercet is a three line poem or a three line stanza within a poem, which can rhyme or not. Haiku are tercets.

And so is this:

He clasps the crag with crooked hands:

Close to the sun it lonely lands,

Ringed with the azure world, it stands.

The wrinkled sea beneath him crawls;

He watches from his mountain walls,

And like a thunderbolt he falls.

- From *The Eagle* by Tennyson

Teaching Tip

As an introduction to writing riddle poems, it would be fun to have a variety of riddles for the kids to solve.

Look for literary devices like rhythm or rhyme in the riddles. They are pretty common.

On the Web

Watch this firecracker jump rope team perform a half time show:

http://youtu.be/MCxGCZZjKMc

Go try it. Then you tell me that's not a sport.

Make up some of your own rhymes and identify the rhyme schemes you've used.

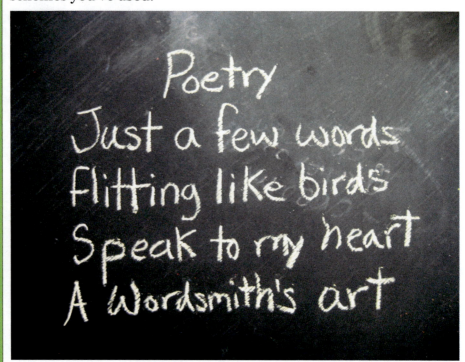

😊 😊 EXPLORATION: Jump Rope Rhymes

Kids have been jumping rope for hundreds of years. Some of the most popular jump rope games involve jumping to the rhythm of rhymes. There are some really famous ones that are full of rhymes. Play these jump rope games and spot the rhymes within them.

Miss Mary Mack, Mack, Mack
All dressed in black, black, black
With silver buttons, buttons, buttons
All down her back, back, back
She asked her mother, mother, mother
For fifty cents, cents, cents
To see the elephant, elephant, elephant
Jump over the fence, fence, fence
He jumped so high, high, high
He touched the sky, sky, sky
And he didn't come back, back, back
Till the Fourth of July, July, July

In "Miss Mary Mack," the last word of each line is repeated. In some other jump-rope rhymes, instead of repeated words, there is counting included in the rhyme. Whoever can keep it going longest without messing up the counting or the jumping is the winner. Here is one example:

Mongols – Caucasus – Gases & Kinetic Theory - Fun With Poetry

Cinderella
Dressed in yellow
Went upstairs to kiss her fellow
Made a mistake
Kissed a snake
How many doctors did it take?
One, two, three, four...

Sometimes the words of jump-rope rhymes have changed a little over time or in different places. For example, here's one that you might hear differently in different parts of the United States:

> *Teddy bear, teddy bear, turn around*
> *Teddy bear, teddy bear, touch the ground*
> *Teddy bear, teddy bear, go upstairs*
> *Teddy bear, teddy bear, say your prayers*
> *Teddy bear, teddy bear, turn out the light*
> *Teddy bear, teddy bear, say goodnight*

Instead of "Teddy bear, teddy bear," you might hear a version of this rhyme that uses the words "Ladybug, ladybug" or "Butterfly, butterfly."

Additional Layer

In the United States, skipping rope was a common way for city kids to play in the streets together from the early 1900s through the 1940s. A special version of jumping rope, called Double Dutch because it uses two jump ropes at the same time, was introduced to the children of New York City by Dutch families who had immigrated to America. Double Dutch later became a competitive sport worldwide.

Memorization Station

Dreams
By Langston Hughes

Hold fast to dreams
For if dreams die
Life is a broken-winged bird
That cannot fly.

Hold fast to dreams
For when dreams go
Life is a barren field
Frozen with snow.

MONGOLS – CAUCASUS – GASES & KINETIC THEORY - FUN WITH POETRY

Memorization Station

Invictus

Out of the night that covers me,
Black as the pit from pole to pole,
I thank whatever gods may be
For my unconquerable soul.

In the fell clutch of circumstance
I have not winced nor cried aloud.
Under the bludgeonings of chance
My head is bloody, but unbowed.

Beyond this place of wrath and tears
Looms but the Horror of the shade,
And yet the menace of the years
Finds and shall find me unafraid.

It matters not how strait the gate,
How charged with punishments the scroll,
I am the master of my fate:
I am the captain of my soul.

-William Ernest Henley

(Written from hospital after the amputation of his leg)

On the Web
Riddles and more riddles

http://www.rinkworks.com/brainfood/p/riddles1.shtml

http://www.funology.com/riddles/

http://thinks.com/riddles/a1-riddles.htm

Jump-rope rhymes are meant to be chanted out loud, sometimes by one person, but usually by a group of kids together.

Have fun skipping rope and rhyming. Can you come up with any of your own silly rhyming poems to jump to?

🙂 🌑 EXPLORATION: Riddle Poems

Riddle poems use the five basic senses to describe an object. Start by writing a lot of objects on index cards, or by placing small objects into a bag. Each person will secretly pull out one object that their poem will center around. Use the five senses to describe it, one on each line, and then end with "What am I?" on the last line.

Here's one about an orange:

> I taste tangy, sweet, and juicy.
> I look like a small baseball.
> I sound as quiet as can be.
> I smell like a Florida orchard.
> I feel squishy, soft, and bumpy.
> What am I?

Sometimes you have to get creative with the sense statements. For example, you wouldn't want to taste motor oil, so maybe you could say "I wouldn't dare taste me" or "The taste would literally kill me."

🙂 🙂 🌑 EXPLORATION: Recycled Poems

Gather newspapers and magazines. This can be done two ways.
1.) You can cut out words and phrases from the newspapers and magazines and rearrange them into poems.
2.) You can take an article and black out many of the words, creating a poem from the remaining words.

Mongols – Caucasus – Gases & Kinetic Theory - Fun With Poetry

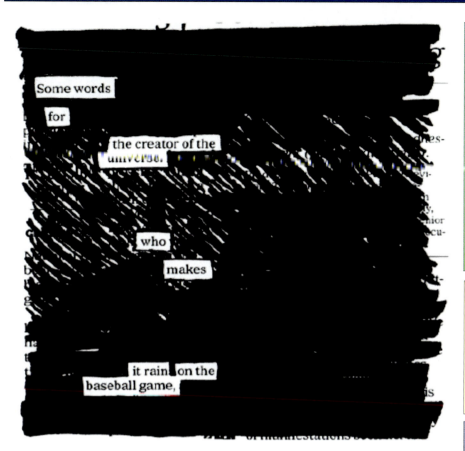

😊 😊 😊 EXPLORATION: Build-A-Poem
Write many words on index cards. You'll want at least 25 words per person – one per card. Make sure to include some nouns, some verbs, and some adjectives and adverbs. It's best if you use some poetry cliché words like love, night, and beauty. Also include unusual words like sled, quirk, serendipity, tadpole, marshmallow, squirming, brunch, and squishy. Once you have your word deck, add 10 extra cards with phrases like looking for, always wanted, it reminded me of, you were there when, etc.
Put all your cards into a hat and draw out several. See what kinds of cool combinations you can make into a poem. You can add extra words when needed, and trade in your word cards if they aren't working together. Keep working at it until you've built a poem that tickles your fancy.

😊 😊 EXPLORATION: The Sound of a Poem
Playing with the sounds of words is the real craft of poetry. Rhyme, repetition, and rhythm are three tools poets use to make their words flow.

Let's read Annabel Lee by Edgar Allan Poe and then look closely at some of his use of these tools. You can read it here and also find it in the printables section at the end of this unit.

Additional Layer
Sometimes poets use sounds in other ways to help their poems, too. For instance, a poet might use very short, choppy words in a poem about anger and very long, lyrical words in a poem about romance. Short and long verses, sentences, and lines are used the same way.

On the Web
Browse some poetry from author Kenn Nesbit with your kids:
http://www.poetry4kids.com/

Additional Layer
When you encounter a non-native speaker you will find that even very fluent speakers have often not captured our stressed/unstressed syllables. Even if all their words are correct, it doesn't sound natural if they emphasize the wrong words.

THE LITTLE dog sat ON THE elephant.

Mongols – Caucasus – Gases & Kinetic Theory – Fun With Poetry

> **Additional Layer**
> This drawing, to the right, of Annabel Lee was done by Manet and published in a French translation of some of Poe's poems. Choose a poem that you like and illustrate it.

> **Additional Layer**
> Alliteration is repetition of the same sound for effect. While rhyming repeats only the ending sounds, alliteration can repeat the beginning sounds or sounds anywhere in words.
>
> Poe uses the repetition of the letters D and S (demons, down, dissever, sea, soul) here, for instance:
>
> *And neither the angels in heaven above,*
> *Nor the demons down under the sea,*
> *Can ever dissever my soul from the soul*
> *Of the beautiful Annabel Lee.*

> **Teaching Tip**
> Make your kids memorize stuff. It makes their minds sharper, more agile, and connects synapses that won't connect without that mental effort.
>
> To encourage their cooperation, try bribery. We do candy . . .

Drawing by Manet of Annabel Lee

Annabel Lee

It was many and many a year ago,
In a kingdom by the sea,
That a maiden there lived whom you may know
By the name of Annabel Lee;
And this maiden she lived with no other thought
Than to love and be loved by me.

I was a child and she was a child,
In this kingdom by the sea:
But we loved with a love that was more than love -
I and my Annabel Lee;
With a love that the winged seraphs of heaven
Coveted her and me.

And this was the reason that, long ago,
In this kingdom by the sea,
A wind blew out of a cloud, chilling
My beautiful Annabel Lee;
So that her high-born kinsmen came
And bore her away from me,
To shut her up in a sepulchre
In this kingdom by the sea.
The angels, not half so happy in heaven,
Went envying her and me -

Mongols – Caucasus – Gases & Kinetic Theory – Fun With Poetry

Yes! that was the reason (as all men know,
In this kingdom by the sea)
That the wind came out of the cloud one night,
Chilling and killing my Annabel Lee.

But our love it was stronger by far than the love
Of those who were older than we -
Of many far wiser than we -
And neither the angels in heaven above,
Nor the demons down under the sea,
Can ever dissever my soul from the soul
Of the beautiful Annabel Lee;

For the moon never beams without bringing me dreams
Of the beautiful Annabel Lee;
And the stars never rise but I feel the bright eyes
Of the beautiful Annabel Lee;
And so, all the night-tide, I lie down by the side
Of my darling -my darling -my life and my bride,
In the sepulchre there by the sea -
In her tomb by the sounding sea.

You already know what rhyme is, but Poe uses it in an interesting way. While we typically focus on the rhyme at the end of a line, Poe also uses rhyme within a single line.

For the moon never BEAMS without bringing me DREAMS

And the stars never RISE but I feel the bright EYES.

Can you spot some of his other use of rhyme?

Repetition is used heavily in this poem. Of course, most noticeable is the repetition of the name Annabel Lee, but he also repeats other important words, sometimes even within single lines.

But we loved with a love that was more than love -

This repetition gives incredible importance to the concept of love, which after all, is the theme of the poem. How many times is the word love repeated in the poem?

Rhythm is the flow of language that is created by stressed and unstressed syllables in poetry. As we read, it can seem like music. We naturally stress certain syllables of words without even thinking about it. Just look at the name Annabel Lee. It flows.

Analyze A Rhyme

Even young kids can analyze poems. Many nursery rhymes have a back story that makes them interesting. Kids can begin to realize that there is more to poems than just what's on the surface.

Go through the steps of analyzing, first telling what you admire, sharing background information, reading it, discussing the meaning, and then spotting literary devices.

An Example:

Read Humpty Dumpty and then go read the Wikipedia article about it.

- Humpty Dumpty has several theories of historical ties.

- There are also several versions of the rhyme.

- It has been referenced in many other stories and poems.

- The theme is that it is difficult to make right something that is broken or wrong.

- It uses an AABB rhyme scheme.

MONGOLS – CAUCASUS – GASES & KINETIC THEORY- FUN WITH POETRY

Great Poems for Primary Students
Picture Books by Dr. Seuss

Nursery Rhymes

The Purple Cow by Gelett Burgess

Limericks, various

The Walrus and the Carpenter by Carroll

Fog by Sandburg

Great Poems for Middle Grades

Talk to Animals by Chief Dan George.

Hiawatha by Longfellow

Casey at the Bat by Thayer

The Cremation of Sam McGee by Robert Service

Stopping by Woods on a Snowy Evening by Frost

The Daffodils by Wordsworth

Great Poems for High Schoolers

Fire and Ice by Robert Frost.

The Old Pond by Basho

High Flight by Magee

Much Madness is Divinest Sense by Emily Dickinson

Passages from Shakespeare

Dream Within A Dream by Poe

Try reading the poem while inserting Annabel Gertrude or even Annabel Theresa. It just doesn't work. We can often identify the rhythm by noting a pattern in the stressed syllables: ba-BUM, ba-BUM, ba-BUM-BUM-BUM. Here are two lines from the poem that I have noted the stressed syllables of:

*I was a **child** and **she** was a **child**
In this **kingdom** by the **sea**.*

You'll read the bold words a little louder and with more emphasis. Try switching them and stressing the unimportant words. It is not only difficult, but sounds wrong to our ears. In English we tend to stress the important words and make the unimportant, small words sound softer.

Choose several lines in the poem and analyze the stressed words to find patterns in his rhythm.

☺ ☻ EXPLORATION: The Rhythm of a Name

In Poe's poem about Annabel Lee we looked at the rhythm of that name. Now we're going to compose some other names with rhythm. Parents often use poetic devices without even knowing it as they name their kids. Watch for alliteration and rhythm as you consider names. For example, parents often choose a letter to repeat, especially for first and last names. I know a family that named all of their children S names because their last name began with an S. Stanley Smither has a natural ring to it because of the alliteration.

Rhythm in names is even more common than alliteration. The middle name Marie is very common because of its rhythm. The 1st syllable is not stressed and the 2nd syllable is, which means it goes with other names well.

Constance Mary versus Constance Marie
Dawn Mary versus Dawn Marie

Does your name have rhythm? Look through baby name books or websites and compose some first and middle names that have good rhythm or alliteration. Often stage names of actors and actresses are more lyrical than their given names.

☺ ☻ EXPLORATION: Share and Analyze A Poem

We've spent a lot of time on the writing side of poetry, but the other side of poetry is the reading of it. Hopefully you've been reading a lot of poems of all kinds throughout this unit – long and short, humorous and serious, form and free verse. Take a close

Mongols – Caucasus – Gases & Kinetic Theory – Fun With Poetry

look at one poem and discover how to read a poem analytically. You can apply these same ideas to lots of poems, no matter the kind.

Nothing Gold Can Stay
Robert Frost

Nature's first green is gold,
Her hardest hue to hold,
Her early leaf's a flower;
But only so an hour.

Then leaf subsides to leaf.
So Eden sank to grief,
So dawn goes down to day.
Nothing gold can stay.

Step 1: Share What You Admire About the Poem
I admire this poem's concise use of words. A gigantic message of the inevitability of change is conveyed in only 8 tiny lines. Beyond that, Frost uses rhyme and alliteration beautifully and uses the sounds of the words to further his message.

Step 2: Give Background Information
- Word definitions are the most obvious background information. In this poem, "hue" and "subsides" are the two words that are most difficult. Discuss what they mean.
- Often poems reference, but don't fully explain, historical or literary references. *Nothing Gold Can Stay* references the story of Adam and Even in the Garden of Eden from the Bible. If kids aren't familiar with it, they'll need to be told the story before they can grasp the full meaning of the poem.

Step 3: Read the Poem Together

Step 4: Discuss The Theme or Message
In Frost's poem, the theme is change. What do people do to avoid change? For example, some people take care of their bodies and exercise to slow the change that comes with aging while other with the same goal have cosmetic surgery. Do either of those things succeed in avoiding change? How else do people avoid change? How about families? Nations? Do any of them succeed?

Memorization Station

The Tyger

Tyger Tyger, burning bright,
In the forests of the night:
What immortal hand or eye,
Could frame thy fearful symmetry?

In what distant deeps or skies
Burnt the fire of thine eyes!
On what wings dare he aspire!
What the hand dare sieze the fire?

And what shoulder, & what art
Could twist the sinews of thy heart?
And when thy heart began to beat,
What dread hand? & what dread feet?

What the hammer? What the chain,
In what furnace was thy brain?
What the anvil? What dread grasp,
Dare its deadly terrors clasp!

When the stars threw down their spears
And watered heaven with their tears:
Did he smile his work to see?
Did he who made the Lamb make thee?

Tyger Tyger, burning bright,
In the forests of the night:
What immortal hand or eye,
Dare frame thy fearful symmetry?

-William Blake

MONGOLS – CAUCASUS – GASES & KINETIC THEORY- FUN WITH POETRY

Writer's Workshop
Write a list poem about things you wish would never change.

Write about something you thought would never change but did, in fact, change. Was it a change for the better? Or did it make you feel sad, angry, betrayed?

Additional Layer
This poem, *Nothing Gold Can Stay*, uses metaphors. Of course green isn't actually gold, that is nonsense. But that's not what the author really means. That is a metaphor; saying something is something else to make a point. It is a form of symbolism.

Emily Dickinson's <u>She Sweeps With Many-Colored Brooms</u> is a metaphor also.

Can you find the metaphor in the first line of <u>A Forest Hymn</u> by William Cullen Bryant?

Step 4: Discuss Meaning Line By Line

Nature's first green is gold.
How can green be gold? It helps if you understand that gold is a symbol of something precious and valuable. Those first shoots and leaves symbolize rebirth and new life and are equally precious, just like gold.

Her hardest hue to hold.
Frost is not speaking literally of holding a color of course. He means that the first green is the stage of growth that goes by the most quickly.

Her early leaf's a flower;
But only so an hour.
These two lines reinforce what Frost has stated in the title and the opening lines: the quick passing of time, the impermanence of the fresh green shoots and leaves of spring. Again, only an hour isn't literal; Frost is using hyperbole to make his point.

Then leaf subsides to leaf.
So Eden sank to grief.
Frost continues in the second stanza with references to Eden ending sadly.

So dawn goes down to day
Every day passes quickly, and we can't stop it.

Nothing gold can stay.
Change is inevitable.

Step 5: Spot Literary Devices
Frost uses alliteration. Can you spot some?
He also uses a couplet rhyme scheme. Can you find his rhymes and give letter labels to the rhyme scheme? (AABB, etc.)

Coming up next . . .

Unit 2-16

China & Japan
Chinese Electricity
Asian Arts

Mongols – Caucasus – Gases & Kinetic Theory – Fun With Poetry

My Ideas For This Unit:

Title: _____ Topic: _____

_____
_____
_____
_____
_____
_____
_____
_____
_____

Title: _____ Topic: _____

_____
_____
_____
_____
_____
_____
_____
_____
_____
_____

Title: _____ Topic: _____

_____
_____
_____
_____
_____
_____
_____
_____

MONGOLS – CAUCASUS – GASES & KINETIC THEORY- FUN WITH POETRY

My Ideas For This Unit:

Title: _____   Topic: _____

_____
_____
_____
_____
_____
_____
_____
_____

Title: _____   Topic: _____

_____
_____
_____
_____
_____
_____
_____
_____

Title: _____   Topic: _____

_____
_____
_____
_____
_____
_____
_____
_____

Mongol Warrior

Mongol warriors were excellent horsemen. The Mongol warriors were lightly armored, but very quick and maneuverable. They were famous for their archery from horseback. They were very skilled with the lance as well. As they conquered foreign people they took advantage of the tactics and technology of those they conquered, learning about siege engines and bombardiers and how to take down the entire Chinese empire with a few nomadic herdsmen.

Layers of Learning

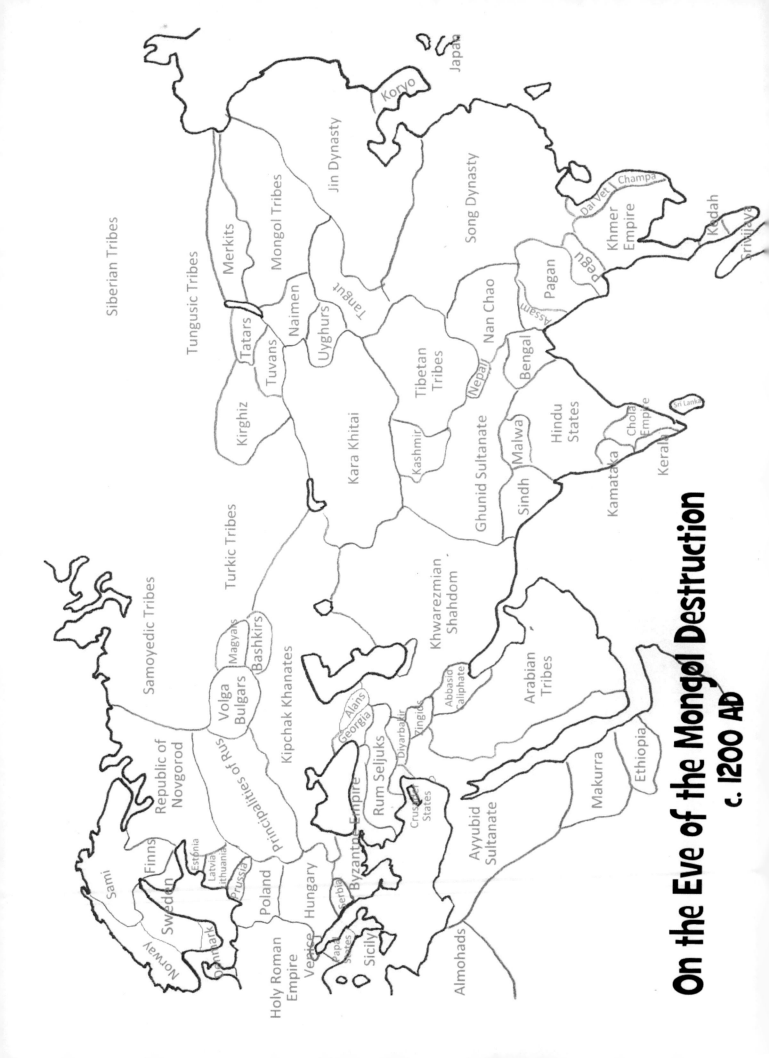

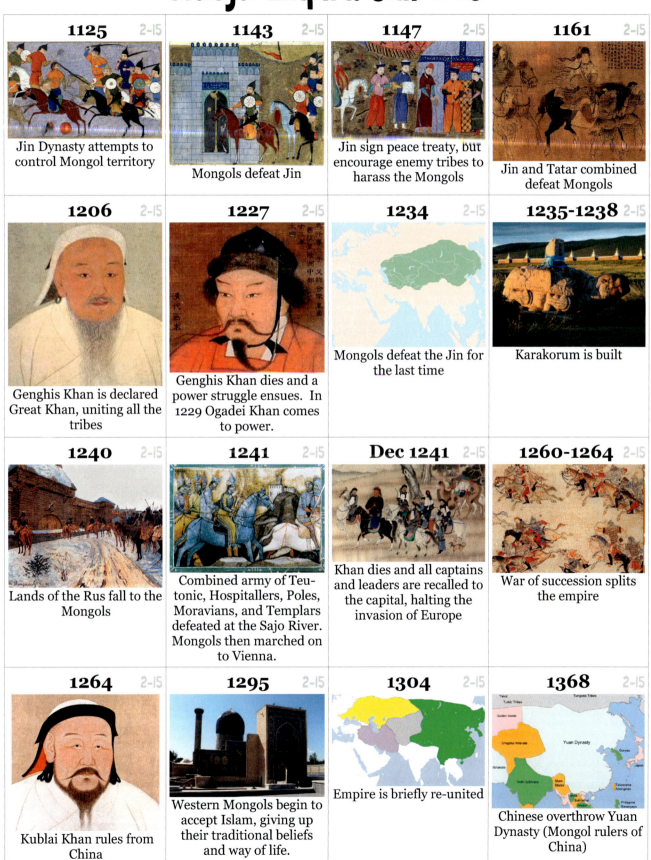

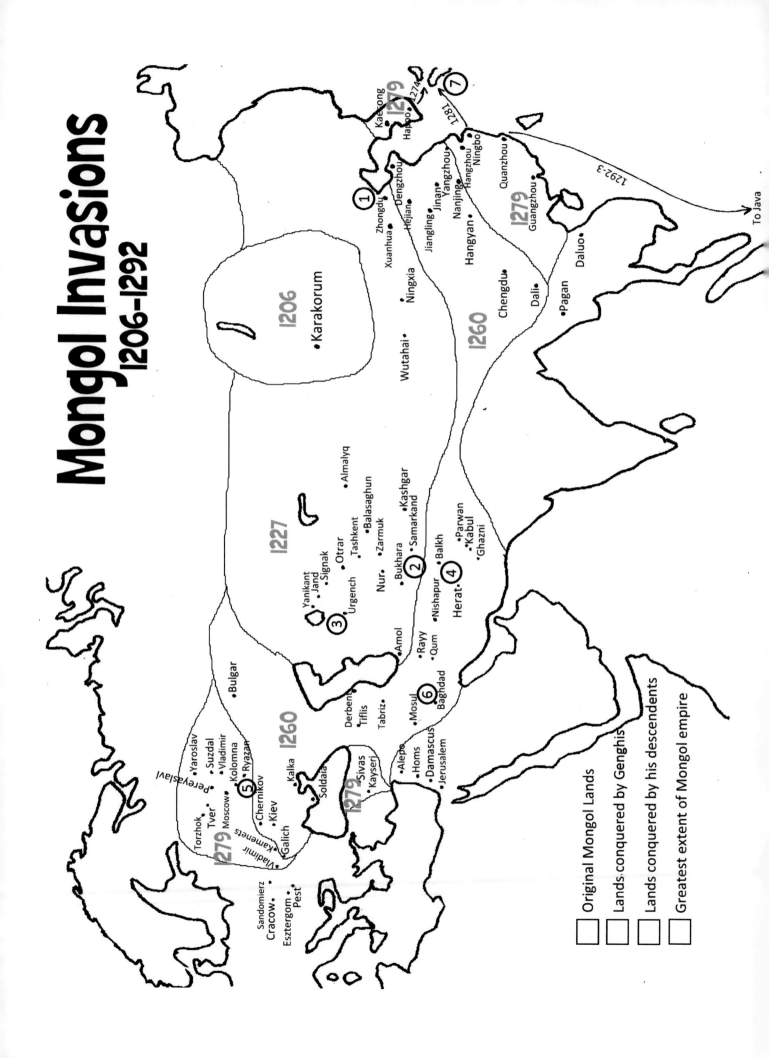

Stories of the Mongol Invasions

1. 1215 Zhongdu (Beijing) The Jin Empire had held off the Mongols for two years. Finally Genghis decided to split his army into three parts to get past the Great Wall. All three spears of the army were successful and broke through the wall. Genghis besieged the city of Zhongdu for months. The defenders ran out of lead for their cannon and had to melt down first, their silver, and then their gold to use as shot. The city was overrun on June 1, the inhabitants slaughtered. The Jin moved their capital south to Kaifing, leaving all the territory north of the Yellow River open and undefended.

2. 1219 The Mongols attacked the lightly defended city of Bukhara first, easily taking the city. They killed all those who attempted to defend the city. The artisans they sent back to Mongolia as slaves. Some of the other inhabitants, especially the older children, they also kept as slaves. The rest they herded into the largest Mosque, told them they, the Mongols, were the scourge of God and the people would be punished for their sins. The Mongols then murdered them all. The city was looted and then burned to the ground. No one remained. The next week they marched with some of their prisoners, mostly children, to Samarkand where they pushed the prisoners in front to be used as human shields so when the people of Samarkand fired their arrows and machines of war they would hit their neighbors from Bukhara and not the soldiers of the Khan. Samarkand fought hard to defend itself, but on the third day they were promised if they surrendered they would be spared. They surrendered. The people were assembled in a field outside the city and everyone was killed. A pyramid of heads was constructed as a monument to the khan's victory.

3. 1220 The city of Urgench was a much more difficult city to take than the previous ones in the region, being built on marshy ground that would not support the siege engines. The people defended their city tenaciously even after the Mongols had breached the walls. They heard what had happened in Bukhara and Samarkand and would not surrender. They fought block by block and house to house. The Khan lost many of his fighting men, especially as the Mongols were not accustomed to city fighting and had no tactics to fall back on. Still, they eventually prevailed. The young men and women were taken as slaves. The artisans were sent back to Karakorum to be slaves for the Khan's capital. And the rest of the city's million or so inhabitants were put to the sword. Not one was left alive. The city was razed, not one building was left standing.

4. 1220 The city of Herat surrendered without a fight after hearing about the fate of Nishapur. Nishapur had fought bitterly for four days and then negotiated their surrender with the promise that the lives of the citizens would be spared. The soldiers and the city leaders knew they would die, but they hoped their deaths would ensure the lives of their people. The Mongols went back on their promise and killed every living thing in the city – men, women, and children, even the cats and dogs were slaughtered. The massacre was overseen by the widow of Tokuchar, wife of a general who was killed in the battle.

5. 1237 The city of Ryazan was the first Russian city to be attacked by the Mongols. The Mongols had discovered that the rivers in Russia freeze solid in the winter and so all their campaigning happened in the winter when the rivers could be used as highways. Ryazan heard of the Mongol approach and begged the city of Vladimir to come to their aid. They were refused, so the city stood alone. They only held out for six days before they were overrun. The inhabitants were slaughtered and the city was never rebuilt. The Mongols then marched on Vladimir, defeated the city in just two days, and killed the king and queen. The Prince fled with an army to fight another day, but they too were hounded and defeated. Every Russian city fell one after the other. Only those who fled the cities and hid were left alive. The Rus became vassals of the Mongols and the Khanate of the Golden Horde for the next several hundred years.

6. 1258 Baghdad was destroyed after the caliph of Persia failed to pay the proper tribute, which included soldiers for the khan's battles and a visit by the caliph to Karakorum. No one thought the city of Baghdad, the greatest city in Islam with over a million inhabitants, with thick city walls and a huge army, could be conquered. A little more than a month after the siege began, the city surrendered. An estimated 800,000 of the inhabitants were slaughtered. The House of Wisdom, the greatest library in all of Islam was burned. Houses, mosques, hospitals, and public buildings were looted, burned, and razed. All this while the caliph watched. Then he was rolled in a rug and horses were ridden over him until he died. The Golden Age of Islam ended.

7. 1281 The Mongols attempted to invade Japan from their bases in China, but a terrific storm blew up and scattered and damaged the fleet so they had to give it up. The same thing had happened in 1274. The Japanese called it a Divine Wind sent by the Gods, a kamikaze.

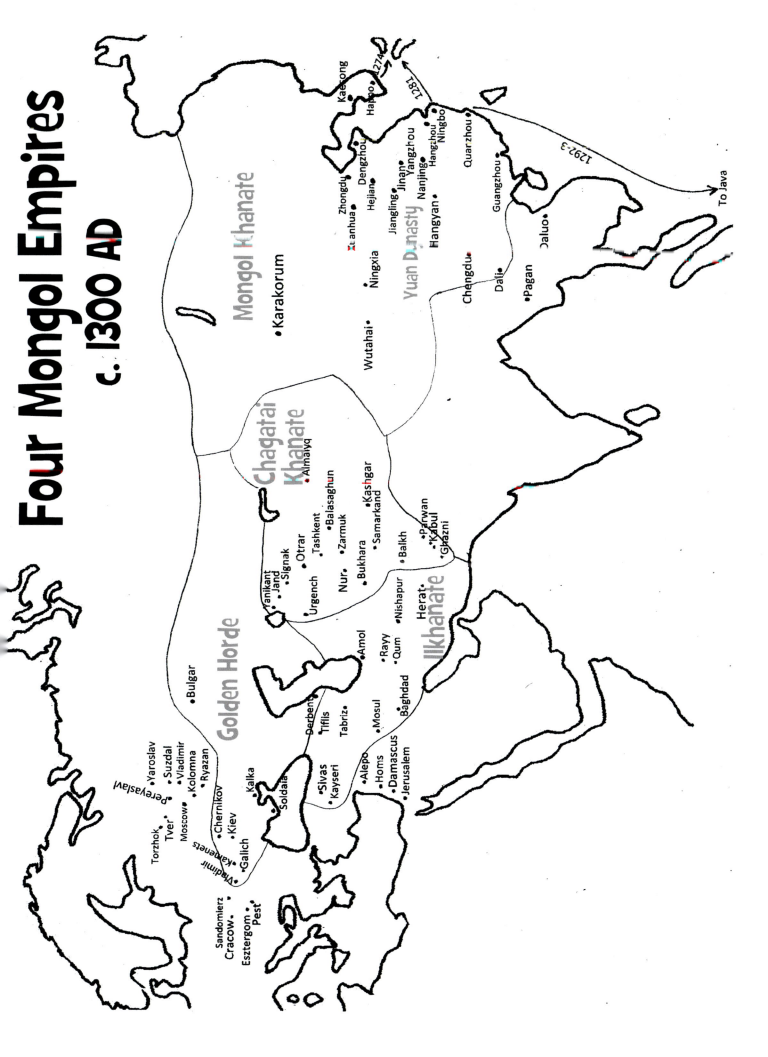

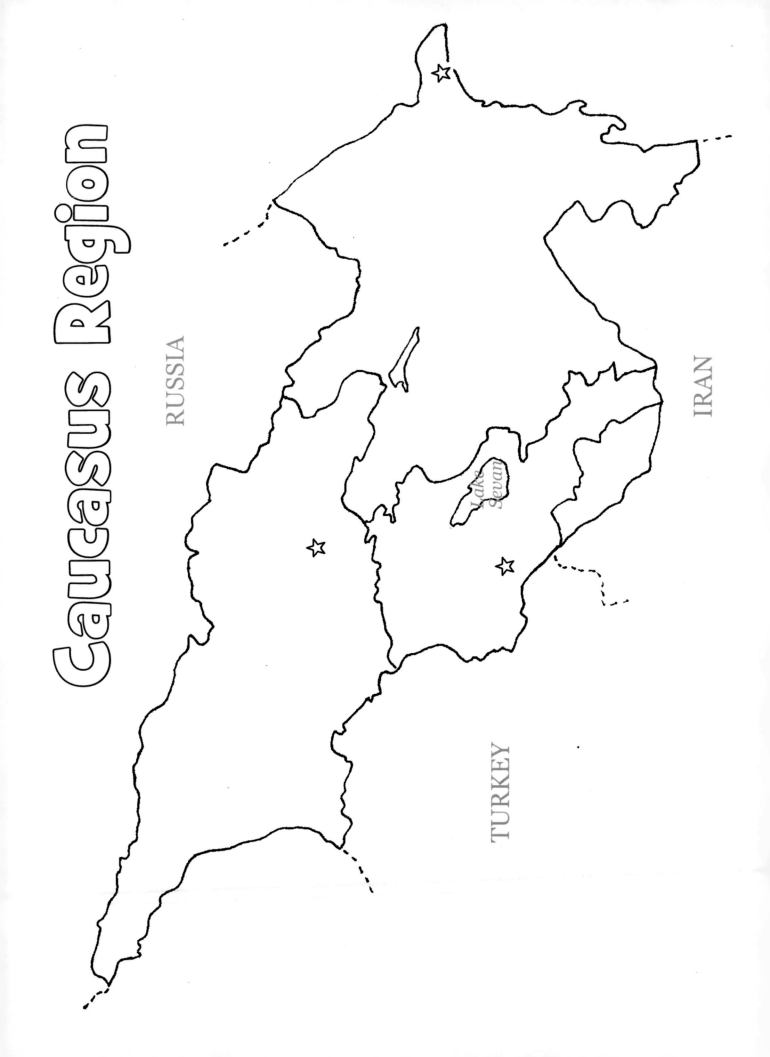

Republic of Georgia

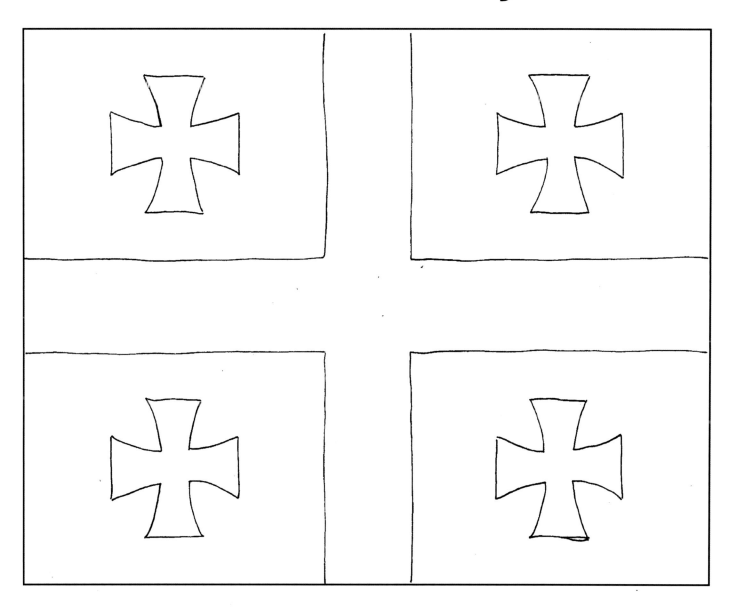

This flag was used by the people fighting for independence from Russia in 1991. It was adopted as the official flag of the Republic of Georgia in 2004. A variation of this flag was used in medieval times by Georgian monarchs. The design is a variation on the Jerusalem cross: a large cross with smaller crosses in each of the four quadrants. It is an ancient symbol of Christianity.

Annabel Lee

It was many and many a year ago,
In a kingdom by the sea,
That a maiden there lived whom you may know
By the name of Annabel Lee;
And this maiden she lived with no other thought
Than to love and be loved by me.

I was a child and she was a child,
In this kingdom by the sea:
But we loved with a love that was more than love -
I and my Annabel Lee;
With a love that the winged seraphs of heaven
Coveted her and me.

And this was the reason that, long ago,
In this kingdom by the sea,
A wind blew out of a cloud, chilling
My beautiful Annabel Lee;
So that her high-born kinsmen came
And bore her away from me,
To shut her up in a sepulchre
In this kingdom by the sea.

The angels, not half so happy in heaven,
Went envying her and me -
Yes! That was the reason (as all men know,
In this kingdom by the sea)
That the wind came out of the cloud one night,
Chilling and killing my Annabel Lee.

But our love it was stronger by far than the love
Of those who were older than we -
Of many far wiser than we -
And neither the angels in heaven above,
Nor the demons down under the sea,
Can ever dissever my soul from the soul
Of the beautiful Annabel Lee;

For the moon never beams without bringing me dreams
Of the beautiful Annabel Lee;
And the stars never rise but I feel the bright eyes
Of the beautiful Annabel Lee;
And so, all the night-tide, I lie down by the side
Of my darling -my darling -my life and my bride,
In the sepulchre there by the sea -
In her tomb by the sounding sea.

XANADU: THE BALLAD OF KUBLAI KHAN
Poem by SAMUEL TAYLOR COLERIDGE

In Xanadu did Kublai Khan
a stately pleasure-dome decree,
where Alph, the sacred river, ran
through caverns measureless to man
down to a sunless sea,
so twice five miles of fertile ground
with walls and towers were girdled round.
and there were gardens bright with sinuous rills,
where blossom'd many an incense-bearing tree.
And here were forests as ancient as the hills,
enfolding sunny spots of greenery.
But O! That deep romantic chasm which slanted,
down the green hill athwart a cedarn cover.
A savage place! As holy and enchanted
as a'er beneath a waning moon was haunted
by woman wailing for her demon lover.
In from that chasm, with ceaseless turmoil seething,
as if this Earth in fast thick pants were breathing,
a mighty fountain momently was forced,
amid who's swift half-intermitted burst,
huge fragments vaulted like rebounding hail,
or chaffy grain beneath the thresher's flail,
and 'mid these dancing rocks at once and ever,
it flung up momently the sacred river.
Five miles meandering with a mazy motion,
through wood and dale the sacred river ran.
Then reach'd the caverns measureless to man,
and sank in tumult to a lifeless ocean.
And 'mid this tumult Kublai heard from afar
ancestral voices prophesying war!
The shadow of the dome of pleasure
floated midway on the waves
Where was heard the mingled measure
from the fountain and the caves.
It was a miracle of rare device
a sunny pleasure dome with caves of ice.
A damsel with a dulcimer
in a vision once I saw.
It was an Abyssinian maid,
and on her dulcimer she played,
singing of mount Abora.
Could I revive within me
her symphony and song.
To such a deep delight 'twould win me,
that with music loud and long,
I would build that dome in air!
Thy sunny dome! Those caves of ice!
and all who heard should see them there!
and all should cry, Beware! Beware!
his flashing eyes! his floating hair!
Weave a circle round him thrice,
and close your eyes with holy dread!
for he on honey-dew hath fed,
and drunk the milk of Paradise.

About the Authors

Karen & Michelle . . .
Mothers, sisters, teachers, women who are passionate
about educating kids.
We are dedicated to lifelong learning.

Karen, a mother of four, who has homeschooled her kids for more than eight years with her husband, Bob, has a bachelor's degree in child development with an emphasis in education. She lives in Utah where she gardens, teaches piano, and plays an excruciating number of board games with her kids. Karen is our resident Arts expert and English guru {most necessary as Michelle regularly and carelessly mangles the English language and occasionally steps over the bounds of polite society}.

Michelle and her husband, Cameron, homeschooling now for over a decade, teach their six boys on their ten acres in beautiful Idaho country. Michelle earned a bachelor's in biology, making her the resident Science expert, though she is mocked by her friends for being the *Botanist with the Black Thumb of Death*. She also is the go-to for History and Government. She believes in staying up late, hot chocolate, and a no whining policy. We both pitch in on Geography, in case you were wondering, and are on a continual quest for knowledge.

*Visit our constantly updated blog for tons of free ideas,
free printables, and more cool stuff for sale:
www.Layers-of-Learning.com*

Made in the USA
Monee, IL
24 December 2020